Lab Manual for
Guide to Computer Forensics and Investigations, Fourth Edition

Andrew Blitz

COURSE TECHNOLOGY
CENGAGE Learning

Australia • Brazil • Japan • Korea • Mexico • Singapore • Spain • United Kingdom • United States

COURSE TECHNOLOGY
CENGAGE Learning

Lab Manual for Guide to Computer Forensics and Investigations, Fourth Edition

Andrew Blitz

Vice President, Editorial: Dave Garza

Executive Editor: Stephen Helba

Managing Editor: Marah Bellegarde

Senior Product Manager: Michelle Ruelos Cannistraci

Developmental Editor: Jill Batistick

Editorial Assistant: Sarah Pickering

Vice President, Marketing: Jennifer Ann Baker

Marketing Director: Deborah S. Yarnell

Senior Marketing Manager: Erin Coffin

Associate Marketing Manager: Shanna Gibbs

Production Director: Carolyn Miller

Production Manager: Andrew Crouth

Content Project Manager: Brooke Greenhouse

Art Director: Jack Pendleton

Manufacturing Coordinator: Amy Rogers

> For product information and technology assistance, contact us at
> **Cengage Learning Customer & Sales Support, 1-800-354-9706**
>
> For permission to use material from this text or product,
> submit all requests online at **cengage.com/permissions**
> Further permissions questions can be emailed to
> **permissionrequest@cengage.com**

Library of Congress Control Number: 2009929885

ISBN-13: 978-1-435-49885-3
ISBN-10: 1-435-49885-2

Course Technology
20 Channel Center Street
Boston, MA 02210
USA

Cengage Learning is a leading provider of customized learning solutions with office locations around the globe, including Singapore, the United Kingdom, Australia, Mexico, Brazil, and Japan. Locate your local office at **international.cengage.com/region**

Cengage Learning products are represented in Canada by Nelson Education, Ltd.

For your lifelong learning solutions, visit **course.cengage.com**
Purchase any of our products at your local college store or at our preferred online store **www.cengagebrain.com**

Visit our corporate website at **cengage.com**

Some of the product names and company names used in this book have been used for identification purposes only and may be trademarks or registered trademarks of their respective manufacturers and sellers.

Microsoft and the Office logo are either registered trademarks or trademarks of Microsoft Corporation in the United States and/or other countries. Course Technology, a part of Cengage Learning, is an independent entity from the Microsoft Corporation, and not affiliated with Microsoft in any manner.

Any fictional data related to persons or companies or URLs used throughout this book is intended for instructional purposes only. At the time this book was printed, any such data was fictional and not belonging to any real persons or companies.

Course Technology and the Course Technology logo are registered trademarks used under license.

Course Technology, a part of Cengage Learning, reserves the right to revise this publication and make changes from time to time in its content without notice.

The programs in this book are for instructional purposes only. They have been tested with care, but are not guaranteed for any particular intent beyond educational purposes. The author and the publisher do not offer any warranties or representations, nor do they accept any liabilities with respect to the programs.

Printed in the United States of America
1 2 3 4 5 6 7 14 13 12 11 10

CONTENTS

INTRODUCTION

The hands-on labs included in this manual are designed to provide additional skills to reinforce the concepts and organization presented in the textbook *Guide to Computer Forensics and Investigations, Fourth Edition*. This book contains hands-on exercises that provide practice in developing the computer forensics skills that are necessary to become a skilled computer forensics investigator. It is designed to support students with a beginning to intermediate level of experience in computer operating systems and networking. It is strongly suggested that students have previous experience in operating systems and computer hardware. This experience should reflect the concepts presented in the CompTIA A+ certification curriculum. For those students who do not have the aforementioned background, a second textbook such as *A+ Guide to Managing & Maintaining Your PC, Seventh Edition* by Jean Andrews may be helpful to understand the computer concepts presented in the labs.

FEATURES

The labs feature step-by-step procedures with image captures to illustrate the concepts presented in the *Guide to Computer Forensics and Investigations, Fourth Edition*. The labs are designed to allow completion within typical class schedules, and they have been tested in classes taught during the past six years. Each lab also features challenging review questions that will require the students to initially install software included on the student data DVD and use the software tools to analyze the evidence files as they answer questions. I have found this strategy works best in a classroom setting with an instructor or facilitator to help guide students.

To help you fully understand computer forensics, this lab manual includes many features designed to enhance your learning experience:

Lab Objectives: Each lab has an introductory description and list of learning objectives.

Materials Required: Every lab includes information on hardware, software, and other materials you will need to complete the lab.

Completion Times: Every lab has an estimated completion time, so that you can plan your activities more accurately.

Activity Sections: Labs are presented in manageable sections. Where appropriate, additional activity background information is provided to illustrate the importance of a particular project.

Step-by-Step Instructions: Logical and precise step-by-step instructions guide you through the hands-on activities in each lab.

Review Questions: Questions help reinforce concepts presented in the lab.

Software and Student Data Files: This book includes a DVD containing student data files and free software demo packages for use with the activities.

The following companies have allowed us to include their products with this lab manual: Technology Pathways (ProDiscover Basic) and AccessData (Forensic Toolkit, Registry Viewer, and FTK Imager). To check for newer versions of these products or for additional information, visit Technology Pathways, LLC at http://www.techpathways.com or AccessData Corporation at http://www.accessdata.com.

SYSTEM REQUIREMENTS

Hardware Requirements (for PC)

- Operating system: Windows XP with SP2, Vista with SP2
- Processor: Intel Dual Core, Core2 Duo, Quad Core, I3, I5, or I7 processors in (x86) or (x64)
- Memory: 2 GB suggested
- Hard drive space: 10 GB
- Screen resolution: 1024 × 768 or higher
- DVD-ROM dual-layer drive

Software Requirements

To work through the labs, you will need AccessData and ProDiscover, both of which are included on the accompanying DVD. The labs included in this book have instructions designed to work in Windows Vista, and they have been tested in Windows XP Professional SP2 (x86), Windows Vista Professional (x86) and (x64), and Windows 7 Professional, Enterprise, and Ultimate in both (x86) and (x64) platforms. The Home versions of all Windows operating systems are not supported, and they may not produce accurate or similar results. Virtualization software such as Microsoft's Virtual PC, VMware, or Sun's Virtual Box will also work well if fast processors and at least 4 GB of RAM are used in the hardware, although the time needed to complete the labs may increase by 25 percent or more.

All the labs using ProDiscover Basic version 4.8 have been tested using Windows Vista (x64) SP2. (Note: There is no technical support for ProDiscover Basic version 4.8 because it has been replaced by version 6.5 at the time of the printing of this book.) The latest version—6.5.0.0—has also been included on the DVD and contains many new features, including support for Microsoft and VMware virtual hard disk images. The ProDiscover Basic version 6.5 graphical interface is nearly identical in function and appearance to the older version 4.8. All the menu items contain the same names and features in both versions except version 6.5 now offers data carving capabilities under the Tools menu. In addition, version 6.5 has replaced the toolbar with icons that indicate the functions without text, and they are in the same location as the earlier 4.8 version (see Figures 1 and 2). The steps outlined in the labs included in this manual can be completed in the newer version using the same procedures.

Please note that software versions are subject to change without notice, and any changes could render some lab steps incorrectly. Instructors may want to use the programs located on the accompanying DVD to ensure that the software corresponds to the activity steps.

Microsoft, Windows, Windows XP, and Windows Vista are trademarks of the Microsoft Corporation. Mac and Mac OS X are trademarks of Apple Inc., registered in the United States and other countries.

CLASSROOM SETUP GUIDELINES

The lab book assumes a base installation of Windows and does not require computers to be networked unless shared resources such as printers, ExamView exams, or Internet access are needed. Lab managers may opt to install all the software included on the student DVD in a Windows computer and use imaging software such as Symantec's Ghost to push the images out to network computers.

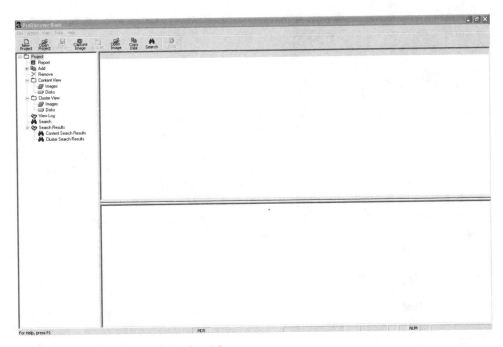

Figure F-1   ProDiscover Basic version 4.8
Course Technology/Cengage Learning

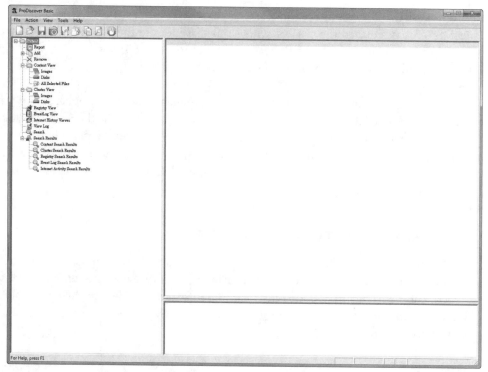

Figure F-2   ProDiscover Basic version 6.5
Course Technology/Cengage Learning

ABOUT THE AUTHOR

Andrew Blitz teaches computer science at Broward College, Edison State College, and Nova Southeastern University in Florida. He has more than 30 years of experience in electronics, computer hardware, data communications, computer forensics, and information security. Andrew has designed and taught online and on-site curricula in computer forensics, networking, information security, incident response and disaster recovery, cryptography, and A+ hardware and software. He has been teaching for more than 10 years and holds a BS and MS in Computer Science and is currently a doctoral candidate in Information Systems at Nova Southeastern University.

ACKNOWLEDGMENTS

I thank Anthony Herrera and Keith Lockhart of AccessData for all their help in providing phone and data images for use in the last labs. Many thanks to Christopher Brown of Technology Pathways for his help and support with ProDiscover. Thank you to the professionals at Course Technology/Cengage Learning for their expertise and commitment to quality. In particular, thank you to Steve Helba, Executive Editor; Michelle Ruelos Cannistraci, Senior Product Manager; Jill Batistick, Developmental Editor; Brooke Greenhouse, Content Project Manager; and Nicole Ashton at GreenPen QA. I also thank the following reviewers: Richard Austin, Kennesaw State University; Jill Canine, Ivy Tech Community College; Michael Goldner, ITT Technical Institute; Wasim Al-Hamdani, Kentucky State University; and Gwendolyn Britton, Western Governors University. Thanks to my friend Amelia Phillips for help and guidance in this project. I also thank my wife Laurie for all her support and help during this project.

This book is dedicated to the memory of Abraham Blitz and Murray Siederman.

COMPUTER FORENSICS AND INVESTIGATIONS AS A PROFESSION

Labs included in this chapter

- Lab 1.1 Installing AccessData's Forensic Toolkit into Microsoft Windows Vista
- Lab 1.2 Installing FTK Imager
- Lab 1.3 Installing ProDiscover Basic
- Lab 1.4 Installing AccessData Registry Viewer

Lab 1.1 Installing AccessData's Forensic Toolkit into Microsoft Windows Vista

Objectives

AccessData's Forensic Toolkit (FTK) combines an extensive array of computer forensics tools into a single stand-alone software suite. FTK allows investigators to analyze a computer hard drive and search for files, folders, e-mails, documents, pictures, and any remaining evidence that might have been deleted or altered. Once the files have been identified, FTK provides a report feature to document the forensic analysis and the procedures used, and help investigators build their case. The FTK suite of tools will be used in many of the lab projects in this book. FTK's graphical user interface is easy to use, and it organizes all digital evidence into buckets that identify the file types, such as documents, graphics, spreadsheets, and so forth.

Forensics investigators need to search large volumes of data stored on different types of storage media, such as floppy disks, CDs and DVDs, flash drives, and hard disk drives for potential digital evidence. In many criminal cases, the suspect might have attempted to delete a file or modify it in some way to prevent other users from seeing it. FTK can recover deleted or corrupted files and display the contents even if they are encrypted with a password. FTK includes powerful search tools that enable investigators to search for specific keywords or number patterns that might reveal telephone- or credit card number–related crimes.

In this lab, you will install FTK and then install the Known File Filter (KFF) database that stores file signatures for popular software products. The KFF Library is a database that provides file signatures for popular software programs, such as Microsoft Word or Excel. File signatures are hexadecimal values obtained mathematically from computer files and programs to determine their originality and authenticity. The KFF file signatures are compared with the file signatures obtained from the hard disk files, and any matches indicate that the files have not changed since they were created by the software vendor. This process allows investigators to concentrate on user-generated files while avoiding vendor software files that do not contain potential evidence.

After completing this lab, you will be able to:

- Install FTK into Microsoft Windows Vista
- Explain the FTK features that help forensics investigators recover digital evidence

Materials Required

This lab requires the following:

- Windows Vista
- ftk-forensic_toolkit-1.81.3.exe
- kff-kff_library_file-29_sep_2008.exe

Estimated completion time: **10–15 minutes**

Activity

In this activity, you will install FTK on a Windows Vista computer.

1. Right-click the **ftk-forensic_toolkit-1.81.3.exe** file in the InChap1 folder on your student data disc and click **Run as administrator** to begin the installation. Windows XP installations don't require this step.

2. In the Open File-Security Warning dialog box, click **Run** to continue.

3. In the User Account Control (UAC) dialog box, click **Allow** to start the program installation.

4. Click **Next** to allow the FTK Install Wizard to continue.

5. In the License Agreement dialog box, click the **I accept the terms of the license agreement** option button, and click **Next** to continue.

6. In the Choose Destination Location dialog box, click **Next** to continue.

7. In the InstallShield Wizard Complete dialog box, uncheck the **Run the Forensic Toolkit** check box, and click **Finish** to complete the installation.

8. Right-click the **kff-kff_library_file-29_sep_2008.exe** file in the InChap1 folder on your student data disc and click **Run as administrator** to run the KFF Library Installer. In the Open File-Security Warning dialog box, click **Run** to continue.

9. In the KFF Database Setup dialog box, click **Next** to continue.

10. In the License Agreement dialog box, click the **I accept the terms of the license agreement** option button, and click **Next** to continue.

11. In the Choose Destination Location dialog box, click **Next** to continue.

12. In the KFF Database Setup alert dialog box, click **OK** and **Next** if necessary to ignore the overwrite notice and continue (see Figure 1-1).

13. Click **Finish** to complete the KFF Library installation.

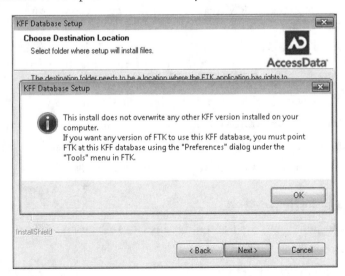

Figure 1-1   KFF Database Setup alert

Course Technology/Cengage Learning

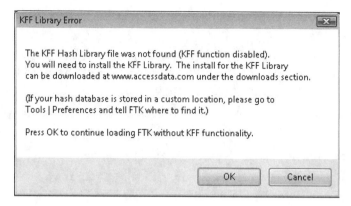

Figure 1-2   KFF Library error
Course Technology/Cengage Learning

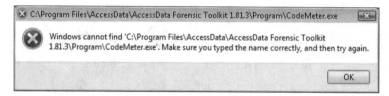

Figure 1-3   Missing CodeMeter.exe file
Course Technology/Cengage Learning

14. On your desktop, right-click the **Forensic Toolkit 1.81** icon, and click **Run as administrator** to start FTK. In the UAC dialog box, click **Allow** to continue to load FTK. Click **OK** to bypass the KFF Library error if necessary. This error is no longer displayed after the installed KFF Library is added to FTK (see Figure 1-2).

15. Click **OK** to skip the CodeMeter.exe missing file error (see Figure 1-3). This error window is normal and appears each time FTK is started.

16. Click **OK** in the AccessData FTK warning box. This warning occurs because the trial version of FTK allows only a maximum of 5000 file items to be added to a case. This message will occur each time FTK is launched.

17. In the AccessData FTK Startup dialog box, click **Cancel**.

18. Click **Tools, Preferences** from the menu to add the KFF Library location to FTK.

19. Click **OK** in the KFF database file dialog box. The database is now added to FTK.

20. The FTK installation is complete. Close the software.

Review Questions

1. FTK is an important forensic tool because it can be used to:

   a. troubleshoot a computer

   b. test a computer's operability

   c. help computer forensics investigators locate potential digital evidence

   d. copy forensic evidence

2. FTK can search for *only* these files:

   a. e-mail

   b. graphics

   c. modified files

   d. all of the above

3. A digital signature or hash is:

   a. a hexadecimal value mathematically obtained from a file

   b. the serial number value of a software program's vendor or manufacturer

   c. the size of the computer's hard disk

   d. the file size of potential evidence

4. Which of the following statements is true?

   a. The KFF is a database that contains the software vendor's product descriptions.

   b. The KFF stores file signatures and hashes of popular software products.

   c. The KFF stores the dates and times of any file changes made to the hard disk.

   d. The KFF contains forensic hard disk information.

5. The KFF is useful in a computer forensics investigation because it:

   a. allows investigators to concentrate on files changed by the suspect

   b. maintains data availability

   c. prevents unauthorized file modification

   d. contains secure cryptographic algorithms

Lab 1.2 Installing FTK Imager

Objectives

Forensics investigators protect the integrity of computer evidence from the time it is seized until the end of the trial by maintaining the chain of custody. The chain of custody must be carefully documented to certify to the court that the evidence has not been altered or tampered.

Forensics investigators duplicate digital evidence by using a bit-stream process called imaging, which duplicates the original evidence and allows agents to examine the copy without the risk of damaging potential digital evidence. The bit-stream process makes an exact byte-for-byte copy of the original storage disk including the physical and logical file locations. This process is important because remnants of deleted files still exist on a storage device until they are overwritten during computer operations. The file remnants can be searched and repaired to recover deleted files and make them readable. The imaging process also generates file signatures or hashes that can be used to identify potential evidence and validate their integrity throughout the investigative process.

FTK Imager can also be used to preview digital files to determine whether evidentiary data exist in the form of documents, graphic files, deleted files, or encrypted files before an extensive investigation is initiated. Although FTK Imager can locate encrypted files, it can't decrypt them and Imager is not designed to facilitate detailed searching. If potential evidence is located, Imager can then forensically duplicate the storage device to safely process the data.

FTK Imager supports the following file systems: FAT12, FAT16, FAT32, NTFS (DOS and Windows), Ext2, Ext3 (Linux), HFS, and HFS+ (Apple Macintosh). Imager can produce hard disk formats supported by FTK, EnCase, SnapBack, SafeBack, Expert Witness, Linux DD, ICS, Symantec Ghost, SMART, and VMware. Although FTK imager can detect encrypted files, it can't actually decrypt them. In this lab, you will install FTK Imager in Windows Vista.

After completing this lab, you will be able to:

- Install FTK Imager into Windows Vista
- Explain the purpose of using an imager tool to copy digital evidence

Materials Required

This lab requires the following:

- Windows Vista
- FTK Imager file

Estimated completion time:	**10 minutes**

Activity

In this activity, you will install FTK Imager into Windows Vista.

1. Locate the **imager-ftk_imager-2.6.0.exe** FTK Imager installation file in the InChap1 folder on your student data disc; right-click the file and select **Run as administrator** to begin the installation.

2. Click **Continue** in the UAC dialog box to continue.

3. In the AccessData FTK Imager InstallShield Wizard, click **Next**.

4. In the License Agreement dialog box, click the **I accept the terms of the license agreement** option button, and click **Next** to continue.

5. Click **Next** in the Choose FTK Imager Destination Folder to accept the default location.

6. When the installation has completed, uncheck the **Run the FTK Imager** check box, and click **Finish** to complete the installation.

7. FTK Imager is now installed. Close the software.

Review Questions

1. FTK Imager can be used to search of all of the following *except*:

   a. files that have been deleted

   b. word-processed documents

   c. graphics

   d. encrypted files

2. FTK Imager is primarily used to produce:

    a. hard disk images that can be analyzed by forensic software

    b. readable decrypted information

    c. computer manufacturer information

    d. file search results

3. Forensics investigators work with hard disk images because:

    a. the image files are smaller than the actual hard disk files

    b. only the image files contain forensic evidence

    c. the image file can be examined without damaging the original evidence

    d. the original storage device cannot be analyzed without the original computer

4. Which of the following statements is true?

    a. FTK Imager can detect and view encrypted files.

    b. FTK Imager maintains the "chain of custody."

    c. The use of FTK Imager is required by law.

    d. FTK Imager supports all file system formats.

5. Bit-stream imaging is the process of:

    a. creating hash values from files on a storage device

    b. extracting readable information from encrypted files

    c. duplicating original data on storage devices for forensic analysis

    d. determining the location of digital evidence

Lab 1.3 Installing ProDiscover Basic

Objectives

Law enforcement agencies, system administrators, consultants, and forensics accountants use ProDiscover to search digital evidence and gather the data needed for any civil or criminal litigation. Additionally, network administrators use the incident response and intrusion detection features of ProDiscover to generate reports on intruders attempting to take control of network resources.

ProDiscover supports FAT12, FAT16, FAT32, NTFS Basic and Dynamic disks, and RAID disk drives used on server computers. ProDiscover also supports the searching of entire storage disks for existing and deleted files, graphic images, Internet history, and Windows registry keys. Additionally, ProDiscover extracts EXIF digital image information that details the camera model, the date and time stamp, the camera shutter speed, camera lens information, and other digital camera information. This information can be useful in identifying the camera that took a particular picture. ProDiscover can also export Windows disk images for importation into a VMware virtualization file. Virtualization is the process of running a guest operating system within a host operating system to allow forensics investigators to view an image as a running computer within a computer. In this lab, you will install ProDiscover into Windows.

After completing this lab, you will be able to:

- Install ProDiscover Basic into Windows Vista
- Explain the features of ProDiscover Basic

Materials Required

This lab requires the following:

- Windows Vista
- ProDiscoverRelease48Basic.zip

Estimated completion time: **15–20 minutes**

Activity

In this activity, you will install ProDiscover Basic in Windows Vista.

1. Copy the compressed (zipped) **ProDiscoverRelease48Basic.zip** file in the InChap1 folder on your student data disc to your Documents folder.

2. Right-click the **ProDiscoverRelease48Basic.zip** file, and click **Extract All** to extract the contents into your Documents folder (see Figure 1-4).

3. When the Select a Destination and Extract Files dialog box opens, click **Browse** to locate the your Documents folder in your computer, and click **Extract** to extract the installation

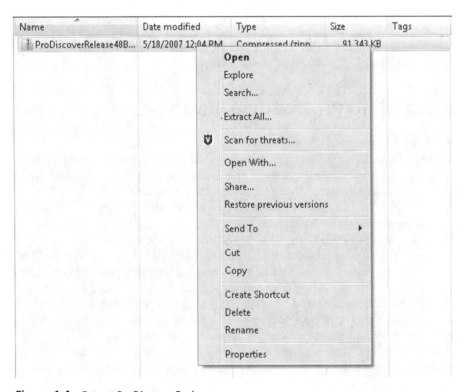

Figure 1-4   Extract ProDiscover Basic

Course Technology/Cengage Learning

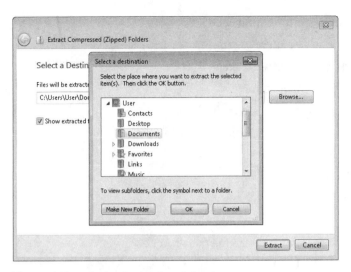

Figure 1-5   Select a destination dialog box

Course Technology/Cengage Learning

files into your Documents (see Figure 1-5). The ProDiscover Basic files are extracted to your Documents folder.

4. Right-click **ProDiscoverRelease48Basic**, and click **Run as administrator** to begin installing ProDiscover Basic.

5. When the UAC dialog box appears, click **Continue** to continue the installation.

6. The Install Wizard starts extracting files to prepare for the installation procedure. This process might take a few minutes to complete.

7. Click **Next** in the Welcome to the InstallShield Wizard for ProDiscover Basic 4.8a dialog box to continue.

8. In the License Agreement dialog box, click the **I accept the terms in the license agreement** option button, and click **Next** to continue.

9. In the Customer Information dialog box, type your full name in the User Name text box. Click **Next** to continue.

10. In the Destination Folder dialog box, accept the default location, and click **Next** to continue.

11. In the Ready to Install the Program dialog box, click **Install** to continue the installation.

12. In the InstallShield Wizard Completed dialog box, click **Finish** and close any open windows or folders.

Review Questions

1. ProDiscover can be used to search of all of the following file systems *except*:

   a. FAT16

   b. HFS+

   c. NTFS

   d. FAT32

2. EXIF contains information such as:

   a. who took the picture

   b. where the picture was taken

   c. the camera manufacturer

   d. when the camera was purchased

3. ProDiscover can search hard disks for the presence of:

   a. Apple Macintosh files

   b. RAID disk data

   c. Linux file systems

   d. UNIX file systems

4. Which of the following statements is true?

   a. FTK and ProDiscover can be used to search Macintosh file systems.

   b. ProDiscover can be used to search Linux file systems.

   c. ProDiscover can create images that will run in a VMware virtual machine.

   d. ProDiscover does not have the ability to produce file hash values.

5. Virtualization is the process of:

   a. running a guest operating system within another host operating system

   b. creating file hash values in ProDiscover

   c. forensically imaging disk drives to obtain potential evidence

   d. decrypting files in ProDiscover

Lab 1.4 Installing AccessData Registry Viewer

Objectives

The Windows registry is the central repository where Windows stores options and settings for hardware, installed software, and computer user–specific information such as account user-names and passwords. The registry is responsible for booting into the Windows environment based on user preferences, and it contains valuable forensic information.

The AccessData Registry Viewer enables forensics investigators to view the contents of the Windows registry and search for specific data such as recently opened files, removable stor-age devices, user account names, deleted files within the Recycle Bin, the registered software owner's name, and other potential evidence.

While the registry includes file information such as date and time stamps, it does not store the actual files—only their physical attributes. Forensics investigators use the Registry Viewer to view registry information not viewable in the standard Windows Registry Editor tool because of Windows security systems.

The registry contains five critical system folders, or hives, that detail the exact system state of a Windows computer at any point in time, including devices such as internal or external hard disk drives that may have been attached and subsequently removed or deleted. Therefore, a forensic analysis of the registry can yield information that files or folders have been deliberately altered or deleted to hide the details of a crime. The registry also contains a history of Internet sites visited, Internet queries performed in search engines with date and time stamps, and a list of all programs installed on the computer along with some owner or user account information. In this lab, you will install the AccessData Registry Viewer into Windows.

After completing this lab, you will be able to:

- Install Registry Viewer in Windows Vista
- Explain the purpose of Registry Viewer

Materials Required

This lab requires the following:

- Windows Vista
- rv-registry_viewer-1.5.4.exe file

Estimated completion time: **10 minutes**

Activity

In this activity, you will install Registry Viewer into Windows Vista.

1. Locate the **rv-registry_viewer-1.5.4.exe** file in the InChap1 folder on your student data disc, right-click the file and select to start the installation.

2. Click **Continue** in the UAC dialog box to continue.

3. Click **Allow** in the UAC dialog box to continue.

4. Click **Next** in the AccessData Registry Viewer InstallShield Wizard dialog box to continue.

5. Click the **I accept the terms of the license agreement** option button, and click **Next** in the License Agreement dialog box.

6. Accept the default destination folder in the Choose Destination Location dialog box, and click **Next** to continue.

7. Uncheck the **Run the Registry Viewer** check box, and click **Finish** to complete the installation.

8. The FTK Registry Viewer is now installed, and your desktop should now include the icons for the Forensic Toolkit 1.81, FTK Imager, ProDiscover Basic, and AccessData Registry Viewer (see Figure 1-6).

9. Close any open windows or programs.

Figure 1-6   Installed software

Course Technology/Cengage Learning

Review Questions

1. The Windows Registry is responsible for:

   a. registering the Windows software with Microsoft

   b. creating the NTFS file system

   c. booting the computer into the Windows environment

   d. storing the list of files and folders on a computer

2. The registry contains valuable forensic information such as:

   a. account usernames and passwords

   b. where the operating system software was purchased

   c. who purchased the operating system software

   d. the actual files located on the computer

3. The Registry Viewer can access forensic information not viewable in the standard Windows Registry Editor such as:

   a. when software was certified

   b. what software is considered illegal   *registered sw owner name*

   c. the version of the HFS+ file system

   d. a history of Internet sites visited

4. Which of the following statements is *not* true regarding what is stored in the registry?

   a. The registry contains information about the Windows operating system environment.

   b. The registry contains user account information.

   c. The registry does not contain password information.

   d. The registry does not contain hard disk information after it has been deleted.

5. The registry is composed of how many hives, or folders, containing system data?

   a. 3

   b. 7

   c. 5

   d. 4

Chapter Two

Understanding Computer Investigations

Labs included in this chapter

- Lab 2.1 Securely Wiping a USB Storage Device
- Lab 2.2 Using ProDiscover to Image a USB Flash Drive
- Lab 2.3 Convert ProDiscover Image to .dd Image
- Lab 2.4 Imaging Evidence Using FTK Imager
- Lab 2.5 Viewing Images in FTK Imager

Lab 2.1 Securely Wiping a USB Storage Device — *Became*

Objectives   *Files taken from another computer.*

WHAT IS THE Recycle Bin file actually here?

There are instances when data must be securely deleted from a storage device to prevent the recovery of sensitive or secret files. Simply deleting files is not sufficient to remove file data because when a file is deleted from a storage device only the pointer to the file location is removed, and the master file table (MFT), which stores the physical location of files within the file system, is updated to reflect the free space. The MFT is a separate structure contained within the NTFS file system, and it is not the Recycle Bin. The actual file information may still remain on the computer even if it has been deleted from the Recycle Bin. Therefore, data may still reside on the computer until all the remnants are overwritten by new data.

In many cases, deleted files may not be overwritten immediately, and forensic software can be used to recover the file remnants and reconstruct the original file. This is known as data carving, and unless the remnants are overwritten with other data there is no guarantee of privacy. Therefore, secure destruction of digital data often requires the writing of useless bits of 0s or 1s to existing files to remove any remnants of perceivable data.

WHICH? WHAT does it do

The U.S. Department of Defense (DoD) standard calls for seven writing passes over existing data before they are considered unrecoverable. ProDiscover includes a disk wipe tool designed to perform a complete erasure of storage media conforming to DoD standards and prevent any forensic recovery. Before digital evidence can be copied to a storage device for forensic analysis, all previous data residing on the device must be completely erased. In this lab, you will take a USB flash drive and securely wipe any data from the device to prepare it for forensic imaging.

After completing this lab, you will be able to:

- Securely wipe a storage device
- Explain the purpose of data carving

Materials Required

This lab requires the following:

- Windows Vista
- 128- to 256-MB USB flash drive that does not have valuable data on it and that can be erased
- ProDiscover Basic (installed in Lab 1.4)
- InChap2 files

Estimated completion time: **60–120 minutes,** (depending on size of USB flash drive)

Activity

In this activity, you will wipe the contents of a USB flash drive using ProDiscover.

1. Log into your computer, and insert a USB flash drive containing any files that you do not need into your computer.

2. Right-click the **ProDiscover** icon on your desktop, and select **Run as administrator** to start ProDiscover. Click **Allow** in the User Account Control dialog box to load the program.

3. In the Launch dialog box, check the **Don't show this dialog in the future** check box, and click **Cancel** to close the open dialog box. Insert your USB flash drive into your computer, and locate the drive letter associated with the USB flash drive in Windows Explorer. Click the **Tools** menu tab and click **Secure Wipe**.

4. In the Secure Wipe Disk dialog box, click the **Disk to Wipe** arrow and click the drive letter that corresponds to the USB flash drive. Verify that you have selected the correct drive letter to prevent the accidental erasure of any other attached storage device. In the Number of Passes selection box, type **7** and click **Start** to begin the process.

5. Click **OK** in the ProDiscover dialog box to bypass the warning that all data will be securely wiped. The Securely Deleting file message will appear in the lower-left corner of the window, indicating the disk files are being wiped.

4 GB, over 5 hours

This process may take **60–120 minutes** or longer depending on size of USB flash drive.

6. When the disk has been wiped seven times, you will see the message "The selected disk has been securely wiped." Click **OK** in the ProDiscover dialog box, and close ProDiscover.

7. In Windows Explorer, right-click the USB flash drive, and click **Format** from the context menu.

8. In the Format dialog box, choose **NTFS** in the File system box, and type **EVIDENCE** in the Volume label box. Click **Start** to format the USB flash drive. Click **OK** in the Format Removable Disk dialog box to start the process.

9. When the format process has completed, click **OK** in the Formatting Removable Disk dialog box, and close the open Format Evidence dialog box. Copy the 11 files from the InChap2 folder on your student data disk. This drive will be your original source of digital evidence; label the storage device. Do not write any more files to it.

10. Close all open windows; you may leave your computer on if you plan to complete the next lab.

Review Questions

SLACK = REMNANTS

1. Which statement is true regarding deleted files?

   a. Deleted files can be rebuilt from existing remnants that have not been overwritten.

   b. Once a file has been deleted from the Recycle Bin, it cannot be recovered.

   c. Once the file pointer has been deleted in the MFT, it cannot be recovered.

   d. The MFT is not updated until all the file remnants have been overwritten with new data.

2. Data carving is the process of:

   a. recovering files that have been deleted but not overwritten

   b. comparing the MFT information to the Recycle Bin contents

   c. erasing the MFT information so that files cannot be recovered

   d. none of the above

3. Under DoD standards, how many passes of writing 0s and 1s is considered secure?

   a. 3

   b. 1

   c. 2

   d. 7

4. Which of the following statements is true regarding the MFT?

   a. The MFT is overwritten each time a file is deleted.

   b. The MFT is updated to indicate free space when files are deleted.

   c. The MFT and the Recycle Bin are the same file structure.

   d. The MFT is not used in NTFS file systems.

5. A DoD secure wipe destroys file remnants by:

   a. overwriting the MFT

   b. writing 0s and 1s to the file remnant locations

   c. writing the information in the MFT to the file remnant locations

   d. deleting files from the Recycle Bin

Lab 2.2 Using ProDiscover to Image a USB Flash Drive

Objectives

When computers are seized during a forensic investigation, the first process of extracting information involves the use of disk imaging to perform a bit-stream duplication of the original storage device. Disk imaging builds forensically legal exact bit-for-bit copies of the original data including the MFT with all the physical file locations containing existing data or remnants and unallocated free space on the hard disk. After the original disk is duplicated, investigators can safely analyze the file structure and recover potential forensic evidence without the danger of destroying potential evidence during the process. Additionally, disk imaging maintains the "chain of custody" by protecting the original data from any changes that might render it legally unusable in court.

ProDiscover supports several types of image formats, including dd, eve, cmp, pdg, and pds, that can be imported into ProDiscover or other forensic analysis software to search for specific evidence during an investigation. In this lab, you will simulate the seizure of digital evidence on the USB flash drive imaged in Lab 2.1 and build a ProDiscover.eve image that will be used during a forensic investigation to search for existing or deleted files. This process is exactly the procedure you would follow during an actual investigation, except that you would use a write blocking device to prevent any changes to the original evidence during the acquisition process. A write blocking device is a hardware or software component inserted between the original storage device and the computer capturing the image to prevent any information from being written to the original storage device. Such an overwriting would violate the "chain of custody."

After completing this lab, you will be able to:

- Explain the purpose of disk imaging
- Perform a bit-stream image of USB or similar storage devices

Materials Required

This lab requires the following:

- Windows Vista
- ProDiscover Basic
- USB flash drive image created in Lab 2.1

Estimated completion time: **10–20 minutes**

USES (... ~)
c. 47.2 MB

Activity

In this activity, you will image the evidence USB flash drive prepared in Lab 2.1.

1. Insert the USB flash drive containing the evidence into your computer.

2. Create a new folder called **Work** in your C:\drive, and then create a folder named **Labs** in the Work folder. This folder will be used throughout the lab book for lab files.

3. In C:\Work\Labs, create three folders called **Cases**, **Data**, and **Evidence**.

4. Double-click the **ProDiscover** icon on your desktop.

5. Click the **Action** tab and click **Capture Image**.

6. In the Capture Image dialog box, select the **USB Evidence** drive in the Source Drive box using the down arrow button.

7. Click the double arrow button to select the C:\Work\Labs\Evidence folder in the Destination box (see Figure 2-1). In the Save As dialog box, type **C2Proj2** in the File name box, and click **Save**.

8. Type your full name in the Technician Name text box, and type **C2Proj2** in the Image Number text box. Click **OK** to continue.

9. When the imaging process is complete, click **OK**. Navigate to the C:\Work\Labs\Evidence folder using Windows Explorer, and confirm that the C2Proj2.eve image has been created.

10. Close Windows Explorer and ProDiscover Basic.

Review Questions

1. ProDiscover supports all of the following image formats *except*:

   a. .dd

   b. .eve

   c. .pdg

   d. .mft

2. The term "chain of custody" refers to:

   a. securing the original storage device in a secure container or forensic locker

   b. maintaining the original storage device integrity by preventing any changes to the evidence

   c. preventing any changes to the forensic duplicate created from the original evidence

   d. none of the above

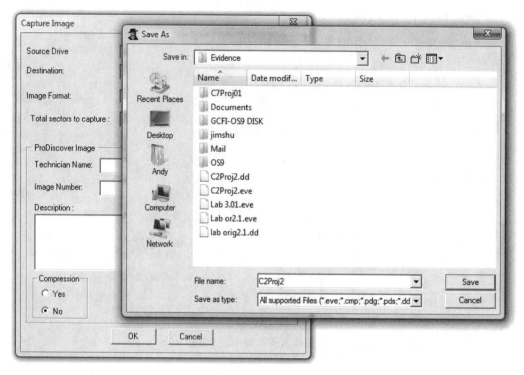

Figure 2-1 Select destination

Course Technology/Cengage Learning

3. Which statement is true regarding a ProDiscover-created image?

   a. The ProDiscover image does not copy the MFT because it is not needed during analysis.

   b. The ProDiscover image copies the MFT and any unallocated free space from the original storage device.

   c. The ProDiscover duplicated image cannot be legally used during forensic analysis.

   d. The ProDiscover image only contains data; it does not contain any unallocated free space.

4. Which is the purpose of a write blocking device?

   a. It is used to prevent any data or changes to be written to the original storage device violating the "chain of custody."

   b. It is used to prevent any data from being written to the forensic duplicate image.

   c. It is used to create file hash values.

   d. It is used to duplicate the MFT.

5. Which statement is true regarding the .eve image file created by ProDiscover?

   a. The .eve image can be opened in MS Word to view its contents.

   b. The .eve image file is not viewable by any software except FTK Imager.

   c. The .eve image can be directly imported into ProDiscover for further analysis.

   d. None of the above answers are correct.

Lab 2.3 Convert ProDiscover Image to .dd Image

Objectives

Forensics investigators may often use more than one software suite of tools to search for digital evidence because the use of multiple software products might yield more forensic evidence than just one product, and they can be used to validate each other scientifically. Different forensic tools produce files that are unique to each product and not normally interchangeable. ProDiscover by default produces images of storage devices using their proprietary .eve format, which may not be usable by another software suite. For example, the AccessData Forensic Toolkit (FTK) does not support .eve-formatted files. However, ProDiscover does have the ability to convert .eve images to other formats, including the .dd format, which is supported by FTK and most forensic software. The .dd format is widely usable by many forensic tools because it also produces a bit-by-bit copy of a file system and it is supported under Windows, Linux, UNIX, and Apple Macintosh OS X.

ProDiscover also supports the conversion of .eve images to ISO, .dd to ISO, and .dd to VMware virtual hard disks. ISO images are archive files of an optical DVD or CD stored in an uncompressed format and usable by many software vendors to create readable disks. A VMware virtual disk can be viewed as a virtual machine that appears as an actual operating system within an operating system. This allows forensics investigators to run the disk image as if it were connected to the original computer. In this lab, you will convert a ProDiscover image to a .dd format that will be imported into FTK in Lab 2.4.

After completing this lab, you will be able to:

- Discuss the conversion tools supported by ProDiscover
- Perform an .eve to .dd format image conversion using ProDiscover

Materials Required

This lab requires the following:

- Windows Vista
- ProDiscover Basic
- C2Proj2.eve file created in Lab 2.2

> Estimated completion time: **5–10 minutes**

Activity

In this activity, you convert C2Proj2.eve to C2Proj2.dd; therefore, this lab requires the prior completion of Lab 2.1 and Lab 2.2.

1. Double-click the **ProDiscover** icon on your desktop to start ProDiscover.

2. Click the **Tools** tab, click **Image Conversion Tools,** and then click **Convert ProDiscover Image to DD** (see Figure 2-2).

3. In the Convert ProDiscover Image to "DD" Image dialog box, click the **Browse** button to locate the C2Proj2.eve file in the C:\Work\Labs\Evidence folder, and accept the default Destination DD Image location (see Figure 2-3).

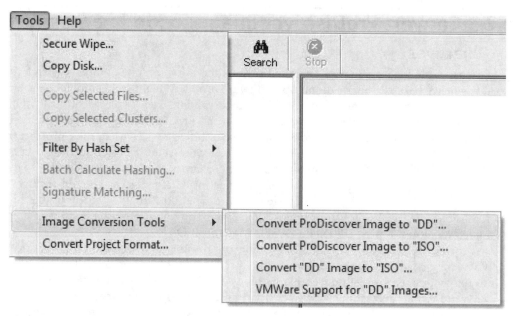

Figure 2-2   Convert ProDiscover Image to DD

Course Technology/Cengage Learning

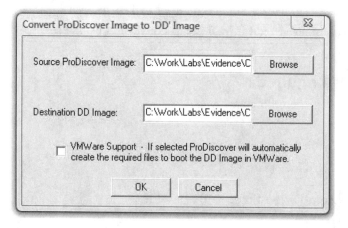

Figure 2-3   Complete conversion

Course Technology/Cengage Learning

4. Click **OK**, and note the green progress bar in the lower-right corner, indicating the file conversion is in progress.

5. When the progress bar has completed, navigate to the C:\Work\Labs\Evidence folder using Windows Explorer, and confirm that the C2Proj2.dd image has been created.

6. Close Windows Explorer and close ProDiscover.

Review Questions

1. Which image format is supported by Windows, Linux, UNIX, and Macintosh?

   a. .dd

   b. .eve

   c. .pdg

   d. .mft

2. An ISO image is an archived file of a:

   a. hard disk drive

   b. flash storage device

   c. CD or DVD

   d. computer's RAM memory

3. The ProDiscover image conversion tool can convert:

   a. ISO images to .dd

   b. VMWare images to .dd

   c. .eve images to ISO

   d. .eve images to .E01 images

4. FTK supports which image format?

   a. ISO

   b. .eve

   c. .mft

   d. .dd

5. Which of the following statements is *not* true regarding the use of multiple forensic analysis tools by forensics investigators?

   a. Forensics investigators should be familiar with more than one forensic analysis tool because they can be used to scientifically verify each other.

   b. Forensics investigators should be familiar with multiple analysis tools because some tools do not support all disk file system images.

   c. Forensics investigators should be familiar with more than one forensic analysis tool because they can maintain the chain of custody.

   d. All of the above answers are correct.

Lab 2.4 Imaging Evidence Using FTK Imager

① what is another imaging tool?

Objectives

FTK Imager is part of the Forensic Toolkit produced by AccessData to search for digital forensic evidence on different storage devices. FTK Imager creates bit-stream images in Raw (dd), Smart, and their proprietary E01 formats. FTK Imager also allows investigators to extract the Windows Registry files from a Windows-based computer and import them into registry viewing tools such as Registry Viewer for password or encryption file recovery.

Unlike ProDiscover, FTK Imager is not optimized to search through large volumes of digital data to locate evidence; instead, it provides duplication and verification features to maintain the chain of custody using MD5 and SHA1 hash calculations. FTK Imager does provide some basic search features, and it can be used to look for deleted files or identify encrypted files. FTK Imager is also available in a "lite" version that can be placed on a floppy disk to make it portable and allow investigators to extract files without booting the suspect's computer. Forensics investigators should also be able to use different imaging software because some have specific features that can yield faster duplications or they may include tools that are optimized for specific file systems, such as NTFS or HFS. In this lab, you will simulate the recovery of files that have been deleted from the original evidence to hide information.

After completing this lab, you will be able to:

- Discuss the image formats supported by FTK Imager
- Perform an FTK imager duplication of a USB storage device

Materials Required

This lab requires the following:

- Window Vista
- FTK Imager
- USB flash drive with evidence created in Lab 2.1

Estimated completion time: **30–40 minutes**

Activity

In this activity, you will delete two files on your USB Evidence drive and image the drive using FTK Imager to produce an E01 image. This activity requires the completion of Lab 2.1.

1. Open Windows Explorer and browse to the Evidence USB flash drive.

2. Delete the **Qtr 1 Emp.xls** and the **Online.doc** files located on the USB Evidence drive. Close Windows Explorer.

3. Double-click the **FTK Imager** icon on your desktop to start FTK Imager.

4. Click the **File** tab and select **Create Disk Image**.

5. In the Select Source dialog box, select **Logical Drive** in the Source Evidence Type, and click **Next**.

6. In the Select Drive dialog box, select the Evidence source drive from the drop-down list, and click **Finish** to continue.

7. In the Create Image dialog box, click **Add**, and in the Select Image Type dialog box, click the **E01** option button. Click **Next** to continue.

8. In the Evidence Item Information dialog box, type **C2Proj4** in both the Case and Evidence Number boxes. Enter your full name in the Examiner box, and type **USB image with deleted files** in the Notes box (see Figure 2-4). Click **Next** to continue.

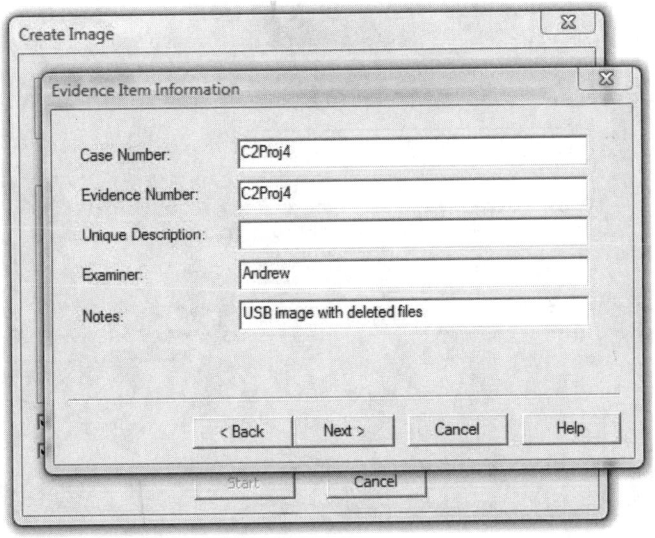

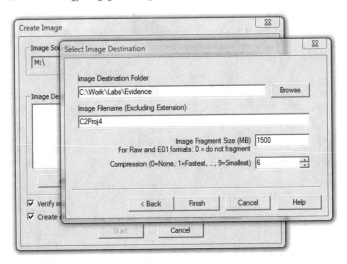

Figure 2-4 Enter evidence information

Course Technology/Cengage Learning

Figure 2-5 Select image destination

Course Technology/Cengage Learning

9. In the Select Image Destination dialog box, click the **Browse** button, navigate to the C:\Work\Labs\Evidence folder, and type **C2Proj4** in the Image Filename box. Click **Finish** to complete the Image process (see Figure 2-5).

10. In the Create Image dialog box, click **Start**.   *3:38 -3:46 = 7mm*

11. When the image process has completed, the results will be displayed along with the computed MD5 and SHA1 hashes (see Figure 2-6). The MD5 and SHA1 hashes verify the integrity of the forensic image. Click **Close** in both the Verify Results and Creating Directory Listing dialog boxes, and close FTK Imager. The C2Proj4.E01 file will be used in Lab 2-5.

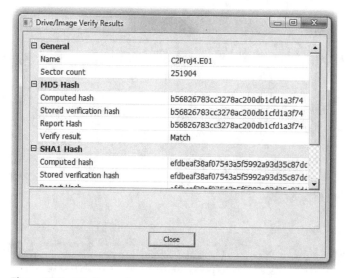

Figure 2-6 Verify results

Course Technology/Cengage Learning

Review Questions

1. FTK Imager can produce all the following image formats *except*:

   a. .E01

   b. .dd

   c. .smart

   d. .eve

2. FTK Imager:

   a. can decrypt encrypted Windows files

   b. is not optimized to search large volumes of data

   c. creates .eve image files

   d. cannot read Windows Registry files

3. FTK Imager Lite is designed to:

   a. be small enough to fit on a floppy disk as a portable imaging tool

   b. decrypt encrypted files

   c. produce only .eve image files

   d. produce only .cmp image files

4. FTK calculates which hash value during file imaging?

   a. MD5

   b. SHA5

   c. DD5

   d. .eve

5. Why is hashing important to forensic science?

    a. Because a hash calculated value can be read by a word processor.

    b. Because the file hash verifies that the "chain of custody" has been maintained during the imaging process.

    c. Because it is faster to search for forensic evidence using hash values.

    d. None of the above.

Lab 2.5 Viewing Images in FTK Imager

Objectives

FTK Imager provides a few cursory tools that are useful for forensic analysis of disk images. These tools include the ability to produce file hashes and view file formats based on their file structure. FTK Imager can be used to perform a quick search of existing and deleted files on disk images, and the data are viewable in their readable state and the hexadecimal bytes written to the disk. FTK Imager displays useful information on the physical and logical data blocks, including bad and unallocated disk blocks that may be useful in recovering deliberately corrupted disk partitions. FTK Imager is useful in narrowing the search scope for evidence because it can be used to quickly see whether any data have been deleted on the disk image. In this lab, you will examine the C2Proj4.E01 image to locate and export the two files that were deleted in Lab 2.4 before the USB flash drive was imaged.

After completing this lab, you will be able to:

- Add images to FTK Imager for preliminary analysis
- Locate deleted files and export them for further analysis

Materials Required

This lab requires the following:

- Windows Vista and Office 2003 or 2007
- FTK Imager
- C2Proj4.E01 image from Lab 2.4

> Estimated completion time: **10–15 minutes**

Activity

In this activity, you add the newly created USB image from Lab 2.4 and look for the two deleted files (indicated by the red X in the file icon).

1. Double-click the FTK Imager icon on the desktop, click the **File** tab, and select **Add Evidence Item** from the menu.

2. In the Select Source dialog box, click the **Image File** option button and click **Next**.

3. In the Select File dialog box, click **Browse** to navigate to the C:\Work\Labs\Evidence folder, select the **C2Proj4.E01** file, and click **Open**.

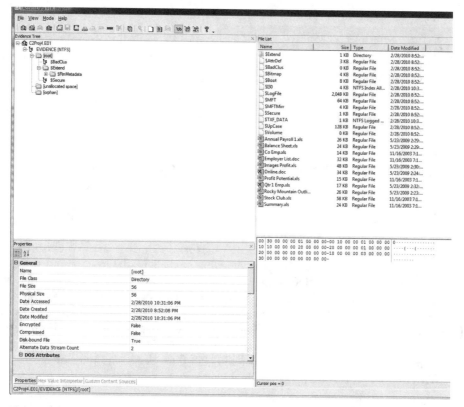

Figure 2-7   Viewing files

Course Technology/Cengage Learning

4. In the Select File dialog box, click **Finish**.

5. In the Evidence Tree window, expand the C2Proj4.E01, Evidence [NTFS], and [root] folders by clicking on the + symbol, and click the **[root]** folder to view the files located on the imaged drive. Note the deleted Qtr 1 Emp.xls and Online.doc files have a red X in the icon placeholder in the upper-right File List window (see Figure 2-7). FTK Imager was able to recover the deleted files from the USB flash drive even though they were not visible in Windows Explorer.

6. In the File List window, Ctrl-click the **Qtr 1 Emp.xls** and the **Online.doc** deleted files to select them. Right-click the second file, and then click **Export Files** (see Figure 2-8).

7. In the Browse for Folder dialog box, navigate to the C:\Work\Labs\Evidence folder, and click **OK** to export the files and click **OK** in the Export Results dialog box.

8. In the File List window, Ctrl-click the **Qtr 1 Emp.xls** and **Online.doc** deleted files to select them. Right-click the second file, and then click **Export File Hash List**.

9. In the Save As dialog box, type **C2Proj4 deleted files hashes** in the File name box. Click **Save**.

10. Answer the Review Questions below, and when you are finished, close FTK Imager and navigate to the C:\Work\Labs\Evidence folder to locate the exported C2Proj4 deleted file named "hashes.csv." Double-click the file to see the Excel spreadsheet listing the two

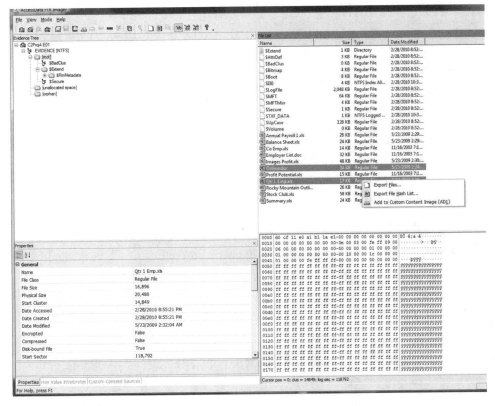

Figure 2-8   Exporting files

Course Technology/Cengage Learning

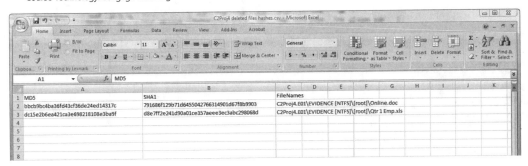

Figure 2-9   Deleted file hashes

Course Technology/Cengage Learning

deleted files and their associated MD5 and SHA1 hashes. Expand the columns if necessary to view the full hash values (see Figure 2-9).

11. Locate the original lab C2Proj2.dd and C2Proj2.eve images. Notice that the image size is just about the same for each image type. Now locate the lab C2Proj4.E01 image, and notice it is much smaller in size. FTK Image creates a compressed image while preserving all the evidence.

12. Save all your work and close any open windows.

Review Questions

1. How many existing Excel files were recovered in the C2Proj4.E01 image file?

   a. 3

   b. 7

   c. 11

   d. 4

2. How many deleted files were recovered in the C2Proj4.E01 image file?

   a. 2

   b. 7

   c. 11

   d. 4

3. What is the file name of the deleted Excel file in the C2Proj4.E01 image file?

   a. Annual Payroll 1.xls

   b. Profit Potential.xls

   c. Qtr 1 Emp.xls

   d. Online.doc

4. What is the name of the deleted MS Word file in the C2Proj4.E01 image file?

   a. Employer List.doc

   b. Online.doc

   c. Rocky Mountain Outline.doc

   d. none of the above

5. How many SHA1 hash files were exported in the C2Proj4 deleted files hashes.csv file?

   a. 4

   b. 2

   c. 1

   d. none of the above

THE INVESTIGATOR'S OFFICE AND LABORATORY

Labs included in this chapter

- Lab 3.1 Processing a FAT16 Forensic Image
- Lab 3.2 Processing a FAT32 Forensic Image
- Lab 3.3 Processing an NTFS Forensic Image
- Lab 3.4 Processing an HFS$^+$ Forensic Image

Lab 3.1 Processing a FAT16 Forensic Image

Objectives

Computer forensics investigators must be familiar with many types of operating system file structures to enable them to search for potential evidence in current and deleted files and folders. Each file system has specific attributes that hold key evidentiary information that may be usable during an investigation. In many cases, investigators need to establish a timeline surrounding a crime to search for possible suspects and establish guilt or innocence. FAT16 was used extensively in MS-DOS and Windows, but because of its limited support for large hard drive sizes, it is no longer used for drives more than 512 MB in size.

After completing this lab, you will be able to:

- Examine a FAT16 .dd image using Forensic Toolkit (FTK) Imager
- Search for existing deleted files and recover the associated file signatures

Materials Required

This lab requires the following:

- Windows Vista
- Microsoft Office 2007
- FTK Imager
- C3Proj1.001 image file

Estimated completion time: **15–20 minutes**

Activity

In this activity, you will add the C3Proj1.001 file as evidence into FTK Imager to perform an initial investigation of the disk image.

1. Create a **Chapter 3** folder in your C:\Work\Labs folder, and copy the **C3Proj1.001** file from the InChap3 folder located on the Student Data disk to the Chapter 3 folder you just created.

2. Double-click the **FTK Imager** icon on your desktop to start FTK Imager. Click the **File** tab and select **Add Evidence Item**.

3. In the Select Source dialog box, click **Image File** as the Source Evidence Type, and click **Next**.

4. In the Evidence Source Selection area, click **Browse** and navigate to the C:\Work\Labs\ Chapter 3 folder, and locate the **C3Proj1.001** image file. Click **Finish** to load the image file.

5. Verify the evidence image file is displayed in the Evidence Tree window in the upper-left corner, and locate the MS-DOS 5.0 text in the lower hex window that identifies this image as a FAT16 partition. Click the plus + symbols to the left of the C3Proj1.001 image and the USBDEVICE [FAT16] device to expand them and view the subfolders. The USB image properties are listed in the lower-left Properties window. Note the attributes listed describe the image type as Raw (.dd) and the original disk geometry as 512 bytes per sector with 251,904 total sectors.

Figure 3-1   File List

Course Technology/Cengage Learning

6. Click the **[root]** folder to display the files located on the USB flash drive image.

7. The files stored on the USB flash drive image and their associated time stamps are listed in the File List window in the upper-right window (see Figure 3-1). Note the files containing a red X in the file icon; these files have been deleted. Click the **!ank.jpg** deleted file to see it in the image viewer.

8. Click the deleted file named **!ank.doc**. It opens in MS Office. Note file attributes associated with each file are listed in the Size, Type, and Date Modified columns.

9. Click the **HEX** button with the eyeglasses located on the toolbar to display the hexadecimal values for the file in the lower-right window. Click the **Bank Location.doc** file in the File List window, and note the file details, including its physical size in kilobytes; the starting cluster and sector are displayed in the Properties window (see Figure 3-2). This information provides the physical and logical locations of the file on the image as well as the d0 cf file signature, which indicates an MS Office Word document.

10. Click the **interior safe.jpg** file, and note the JFIF file signature indicating a JPEG graphic image file. File signatures are useful in identifying file types when the file extensions have been deleted or modified to hide the file during an investigation (see Figure 3-3).

11. Click the **Eyeglasses** button on the toolbar to view the image in the viewer. Select each file, including the deleted files, to view them in the viewer along with their associated properties.

12. Expand the **[root]** folder by clicking the **+** next to the folder, and note the file structure located in the root directory.

13. Leave FTK Imager open as you complete the review questions below. Click the **File** menu, and select **Exit** to close FTK Imager after you complete the questions.

Figure 3-2 File details

Course Technology/Cengage Learning

Figure 3-3 Graphic image file

Course Technology/Cengage Learning

Review Questions

1. How many existing MS Word documents are stored in the FAT16 image?

   a. 2

   b. 6

   c. 13

   d. 4

2. How many deleted MS Word documents are stored in the FAT16 image?

   a. 3

   b. 1

   c. 6

   d. 13

3. How many existing graphics images are stored in the FAT16 image?

   a. 13

   b. 6

   c. 9

   d. 10

4. What is depicted in the deleted graphics image?

   a. a picture of a red brick building

   b. a picture of a lobby

   c. a picture of a lock with two keys

   d. a picture of a security guard

5. What is the Start Sector of the deleted graphics image file?

   a. 876

   b. 848

   c. 107

   d. 1,264

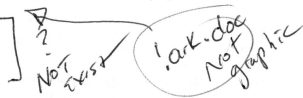

Lab 3.2 Processing a FAT32 Forensic Image

Objectives

FAT32 is an improved version of the FAT16 file system that uses a 32-bit address to allocate disk space. Its 32-bit file system enables it to support the large disk capacities found on modern computers, and it is also supported by Linux, Macintosh OS X, as well as Windows 98 and higher operating systems. The FAT32 file system also supports file name sizes up to 255 characters long, providing a more convenient file-naming structure.

After completing this lab, you will be able to:

- Examine a FAT32 .dd image using FTK Imager
- Identify a FAT32 file system signature

Materials Required

This lab requires the following:

- Windows Vista
- FTK Imager
- C3Proj2.001 image file

Estimated completion time: **15–20 minutes**

Activity

In this activity, you will add the C3Proj2.001 file as evidence into the FTK Imager to perform an initial investigation of the disk image.

1. Copy the **C3Proj2.001** image file from the InChap3 folder on the Student Data disk to your C:\Work\Labs\Chapter3 folder.

2. Double-click the **FTK Imager** icon on your desktop to start FTK Imager.

3. Click the **File** menu tab and select **Add Evidence Item**.

4. In the Select Source dialog box, click **Image File** as the Source Evidence Type, and click **Next**.

5. In the Evidence Source Selection area, click **Browse** and navigate to the **C3Proj2.001** image file located in the C:\Work\Labs\Chapter3 folder. Click **Finish** to load the image file.

6. Click the + symbols to expand the C3Proj2.001 image file and the USBDEVICE [FAT32] device. The USB image properties are listed in the lower-left Properties window. Note the Disk attributes, which describe the image type as Raw (.dd) and the original disk geometry as 512 bytes per sector with 249,341 total sectors.

7. Click the **[root]** folder to display the files located on the USB flash drive image. The files stored on the USB flash drive image and their associated time stamps are listed in the File List window in the upper-right window. Note the files containing a red X in the file icon indicate that the files were deleted from the USB flash drive. Note that the USBDEVICE [FAT32] device is formatted in a FAT32 file system as indicated by the [FAT32] description in the name.

8. Click the **Bank Location.doc** file, and view the file details describing its physical size in kilobytes (see Figure 3-4). Note the starting cluster and sector are displayed in the Properties window. This information provides the physical and logical locations of the file on the image, as well as the file signature indicating an MS Office Word document in the first 2 bytes. The file signature and file size are the same as the FAT16 file system; however, the file start locations are different from the FAT16 file system. Compare Figure 3-4 with Figure 3-2 to see the similarities and differences between the FAT32 and FAT16 file systems allocating space for the Bank Location.doc file.

9. Click the **HEX** button with the eyeglasses icon located in the toolbar, and click the **interior safe.jpg** file in the File List window. Note the JFIF file signature is similar to the FAT16 JPEG file signature. Compare the file attributes with the Figure 3-3 image of the same file on the FAT16 device.

Figure 3-4   FAT32 image

Course Technology/Cengage Learning

10. Click the **Eyeglasses** button on the toolbar to view the image in the viewer. The images are exactly the same as the FAT16 image with the same file name, except for the Start Cluster and Sector locations.

11. Leave FTK Imager open as you complete the lab questions below. Click the **File** menu, and select **Exit** to close FTK Imager after you complete the questions.

Review Questions

1. How many clusters are contained in the FAT32 image?

   a. 120,229

   b. 120,574

   c. 2,048

   d. 8,192

2. How many files (existing and deleted) are contained in the FAT32 image?

   a. 9

   b. 11

   c. 16

   d. 10

3. How many existing MS Excel files are contained in the FAT32 image?

   a. 3

   b. 2

   c. 1

   d. 13

1 deleted

2 real

4. What is the Start Sector number of the deleted MS Excel file?

   a. 8,814

   b. 8,616

   c. 8,306

   d. 8,262

5. What is the FAT32 drive Volume Serial Number?

   a. 929E-685C

   b. 2,048

   c. 99E-0766

   d. 249,341

Lab 3.3 Processing an NTFS Forensic Image

Objectives

NTFS is a file system supported by Windows NT, 2000, XP, Vista, and Windows 7. It is also used by all the Windows Server operating systems because it supports additional file attributes such as compression and encryption. Operating systems such as MS-DOS; Windows 95, 98, and ME; and UNIX do not support the NTFS file system; therefore, any files located on an NTFS partition would not be viewable.

NTFS is considered more reliable than FAT16 and FAT32 because of the duplicate master file tables, which support redundancy. NTFS supports file encryption based on user account information so that multiple users on the same computer will not see each other's encrypted files.

After completing this lab, you will be able to:

- Examine an NTFS .dd image using FTK Imager
- Identify an NTFS file system signature

Materials Required

This lab requires the following:

- Windows Vista
- FTK Imager
- C3Proj3.001 image file

Estimated completion time: **15–20 minutes**

Activity

In this activity, you will add the C3Proj3.001 file as evidence into FTK Imager to perform an initial investigation of the disk image.

1. Copy the **C3Proj3.001** image file from the InChap3 folder on the Student Data disk to your C:\Work\Labs\Chapter3 folder.

2. Double-click the **FTK Imager** icon on your desktop to start FTK Imager.

3. Click the **File** tab and select **Add Evidence Item**.

4. In the Select Source dialog box, click **Image File** as the Source Evidence Type, and click **Next**.

5. In the Evidence Source Selection area, click **Browse** and navigate to the **C3Proj3.001** image file located in the C:\Work\Labs\Chapter3 folder. Click **Finish** to load the image file.

6. Click the + symbols to expand the C3Proj3.001 image file and the USBDEVICE [NTFS] device. The USB image properties are listed in the lower-left Properties window; note the Disk attributes that describe the image type as Raw (.dd) and the original disk geometry as 512 bytes per sector with 51,904 total sectors.

7. Click the **[root]** folder to display the files located on the USB flash drive image. Note that the USBDEVICE [NTFS] device is formatted in the NTFS file system as indicated by the [NTFS] description in the name. The NTFS file system contains additional file structures in the [root] for bad cluster identification ($BadClus) and two copies of the Master File Table ($MFT and $MFTMIrr) (see Figure 3-5).

Figure 3-5   NTFS image

Course Technology/Cengage Learning

8. The files stored on the USB flash drive image and their associated time stamps are listed in the File List window in the upper-right window. Note the files containing a red X in the file icon, indicating that the files were deleted from the USB flash drive. View each file by clicking it, and also look at the deleted files. Note that NTFS contains a Date Accessed field in addition to the Date Created and Date Modified fields.

9. Click the **HEX** button with the eyeglasses located in the toolbar, and   click the **Bank Location.doc** file. Note the file details, including its physical size in kilobytes; the starting cluster and sector are displayed in the Properties window. Use the scroll bar on the right side of the Properties window to see all the additional file attributes.

10. Click the **interior safe.jpg** file, and note that the JFIF file signature is similar to the FAT16 and FAT32 JPEG file signatures. Also note that NTFS supports EXIF file data, which provide information on the digital camera's model number, manufacturer, shutter speed, lens aperture, and ISO speed. This information can be very useful to forensics investigators.

11. Leave FTK Imager open as you complete the lab questions below. Click **File** menu, and select **Exit** to close FTK Imager after you complete the questions.

Review Questions

1. What is the cluster size in the NTFS file system?

   a. 2,048

   b. 1,024

   c. 4,096

   d. 31,487

2. What is the volume serial number for this image?

   a. E16-566

   b. E6FE-1C5F

   c. 2,048

   d. 4,096

3. What time was the bank.jpg image deleted?

   a. 2:15:31 AM

   b. 4:59:14 PM

   c. 12:37:00 PM

   d. 12:37:21 PM

4. What is the physical size of the deleted mark.doc file?

   a. 31,744

   b. 32,768

   c. 14,808

   d. 118,464

5. What additional folder is contained in the NTFS image but was not found in either the FAT16 or FAT32 images?

   a. [unallocated space]

   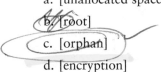 b. [root]

   c. [orphan]

   d. [encryption]

Lab 3.4 Processing an HFS⁺ Forensic Image

Objectives

HFS⁺ is the file system used by Macintosh computers running OS X 10.4 and higher. Unlike NTFS, HFS⁺ is a file system that maintains a journal to keep track of file changes attempted but not completed because of file errors or hard disk issues. The journal allows the file system to recover from sudden disk crashes or power loss during a write operation. HFS⁺ is similar to NTFS in providing excellent file recovery after file corruption or accidental file deletion.

After completing this lab, you will be able to:

- Add an HFS⁺ image to FTK for processing
- Explain the difference between HFS⁺ and Windows file systems
- Find the location of deleted files

Materials Required

This lab requires the following:

- Windows XP or Vista
- FTK Imager
- C3Proj4.001 image file

Estimated completion time: **10–15 minutes**

Activity

In this activity, you will add the C3Proj4.001 file as evidence into FTK Imager to perform an initial investigation of the disk image.

1. Copy the **C3Proj4.001** image file from the InChap3 folder on the Student Data disk to your C:\Work\Labs\Chapter3 folder.

2. Click the **FTK Imager** icon on your desktop.

3. Click the **File** menu tab, and select **Add Evidence Item**.

4. In the Select Source dialog box, click **Image File** as the Source Evidence Type, and click **Next**.

5. In the Evidence Source Selection area, click **Browse** and navigate to the **C3Proj4.001** image file located in the C:\Work\Labs\Chapter3 folder. Click **Finish** to load the image file.

6. Click the + symbols to expand the **C3Proj4.001** image file and the USBDEVICE [HFS⁺] device. The USB image properties are listed in the lower-left Properties window; note the Disk attributes that describe the image type as Raw (.dd) and the original disk geometry as 512 bytes per sector with 249,228 total sectors.

7. Click the **USBDevice** folder to display the files located on the USB flash drive image. Note the UNIX Permissions for the USBDEVICE folder. These include, read, write, delete, and modify. Note the missing [root] folder and the additional folders supporting the journaling of file transactions (see Figure 3-6).

8. Double-click the **.Trashes** folder, and double-click the **501** folder. Note the same three deleted files; however, HFS⁺ does not place a red X in the icon to indicate that they were deleted. The files are only listed in the .Trashes folder.

9. View each file by clicking it, and also look at the deleted images in the viewer. Note that HFS+ also contains a Date Accessed field in addition to the Date Created and Date Modified fields.

10. Click the **USBDevice** folder, and click the **HEX** button with the eyeglasses located on the toolbar to display the hexadecimal values. Click the **Bank Location.doc** file, and use the scroll bar on the right of the Properties window to see the file attributes. This information provides the physical and logical locations of the file on the image similar to the attributes you viewed in Labs 3.2 and 3.3; however, HFS⁺ has several attributes not common to FAT16, FAT32, and NTFS.

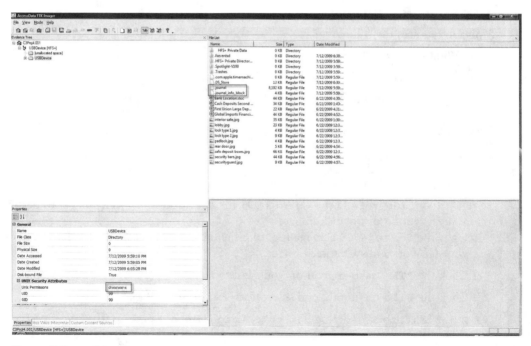

Figure 3-6   HFS⁺ image

Course Technology/Cengage Learning

11. Click the **interior safe.jpg** file, and note the JFIF file signature is similar to the FAT16, FAT32, and NTFS JPEG file signatures. Also note that HFS⁺ also supports EXIF file data in a similar fashion to the other file systems you have examined.

12. Leave FTK Imager open as you complete the lab questions below. Click **File** menu, and select **Exit** to close FTK Imager after you complete the questions.

Review Questions

1. What is the cluster size of the HFS+ USBDEVICE?

    a. 1,024

    b. 2,048

    c. 4,096

    d. 3,077

2. How many clusters are contained in the HFS⁺ image file?

    a. 31,153

    b. 21,866

    c. 28,099

    d. 249,228

3. What date was the HFS⁺ partition created?

    a. 6/22/2009

    b. 7/16/2009

    c. 7/12/2009

    d. 7/14/2009

4. What folder structure is not contained in HFS⁺ but can be found in FAT16, FAT32, and NTFS?

    a. [orphan]

    b. [USB]

    c. [unallocated space]

    d. [root]

5. In what parent folder can the deleted files be found?

    a. .Trashes

    b. [root]

    c. [orphan]

    d. [unallocated space]

1. FTR IMMER

2. PARTION COPIED to Thumb

3. Physical — sh

TAT
MFS

DATA ACQUISITION

Labs included in this chapter

- Lab 4.1 Data Acquisition in ProDiscover

- Lab 4.2 Viewing an NTFS Image in ProDiscover

- Lab 4.3 Adding Forensic Evidence to Forensic Toolkit 1.81

- Lab 4.4 Viewing an NTFS Image in Forensic Toolkit 1.81

Lab 4.1 Data Acquisition in ProDiscover

Objectives

During the process of seizing a storage device, investigators use imaging tools to create a forensic copy that can be safely analyzed without the danger of damaging or deleting potential evidence. The forensic image is an exact copy of the original evidence, including any unallocated space or bad clusters. In addition, the imaging process creates a hash signature of the original and the duplicated copy to validate the scientific imaging process and ensure that no file has been omitted or changed in any way. The two hash signatures are compared with each other, and if they match, the copy is considered legally identical to the original. The forensic copy maintains the chain of custody from the time the seized device was imaged until the end of the investigation. In addition, the information obtained by the various tools applied to the evidence will be listed in a report that can be examined during the trial by investigators and court personnel.

In this lab, you will add the C4Proj1.dd image file to ProDiscover and perform an initial investigation of the acquired evidence.

After completing this lab, you will be able to:

- Add a .dd image to ProDiscover and search for potential evidence

- Bookmark suspicious files and create a report in ProDiscover

Materials Required

This lab requires the following:

- Windows Vista
- C4Proj1.dd file
- ProDiscover Basic

Estimated completion time: **15–20 minutes**

Activity

In this activity, you will add an image file of a storage device into ProDiscover Basic.

1. Double-click the **ProDiscover** icon located on your desktop.

2. Click the **File** tab and click **New Project**.

3. In the New Project dialog box, type **C4Lab1** into the Project Number and Project File Name boxes, and click **OK**.

4. Click the **Action** tab and click **Add**; then in the submenu, click **Image File**.

5. In the Open dialog box, browse to the location of the C4Proj1.dd file in the InChap4 folder on the student data disk, and click **OPEN**.

6. Expand the **Images** icon located under the **Content View** by clicking on the + symbol, and click the **C4Proj1.dd** image icon.

7. Note that the files displayed in the upper-right window represent the root directory listing of the imaged storage device. Click the + symbol to expand the Image file, and see the folder below containing all the files on the device (see Figure 4-1).

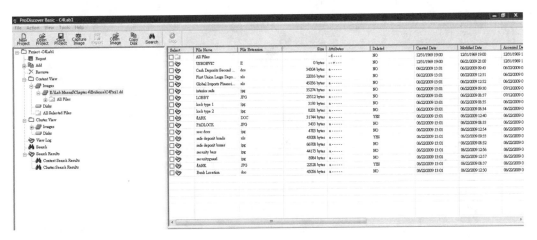

Figure 4-1 Root directory listing

Course Technology/Cengage Learning

8. Deleted files are represented by a red X in the icon next to the check box. Click the first two deleted files, and view the text along with the formatting structure in the lower-right window. The first deleted file is an MS Word document, and the second file is an MS Excel file. The last deleted file is a .jpg image file, and it must be viewed using a graphic image viewer.

9. Click the check box next to the first deleted file, type **Deleted** file in the Add Comment dialog box, and click **OK**. Repeat this process for the other two deleted files. You should see check marks next to each of the files.

10. Click the **Tools** tab, and select **Batch Calculate Hashing**. Click **Yes** in the ProDiscover dialog box to disregard the notification.

11. Click the **View** tab, and click **Gallery View** to display the graphic images (see Figure 4-2).

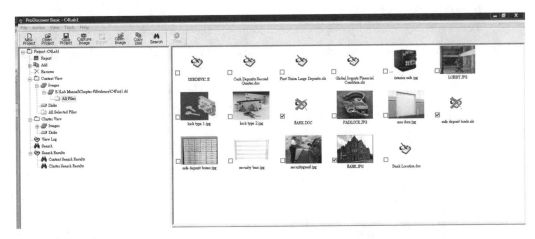

Figure 4-2 Graphic images

Course Technology/Cengage Learning

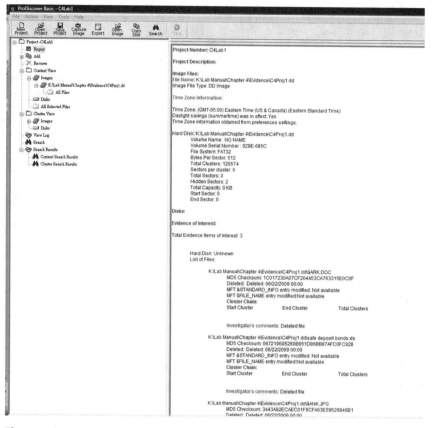

Figure 4-3   Report

Course Technology/Cengage Learning

12. Click the **View** tab, and click **Report** to display the results of your initial investigation of this evidence (see Figure 4-3).

13. Leave the report window open as you complete the following lab questions.

14. Click the **File** tab and select **Exit**. Click **No** in the ProDiscover dialog box to close ProDiscover.

Review Questions

1. What is the file system used in this image?

   a. HFS+

   b. FAT16

   c. FAT32

   d. NTFS

2. What is the time zone where this image was located?

   a. Eastern

   b. Central

   c. Pacific

   d. Mountain

3. What is the total number of clusters contained in this image?

   a. 512

   b. 120574

   c. 64

   d. 128

4. How many hidden sectors are contained in this image?

   a. 4

   b. 1

   c. 3

   d. 2

5. On what date were the three files deleted?

   a. 07/06/2005

   b. 06/22/2009

   c. 05/18/2009

   d. 06/14/2009

Lab 4.2 Viewing an NTFS Image in ProDiscover

Objectives

The New Technology File System (NTFS) was first available in Windows NT, and it is supported in Windows 2000, XP, Vista, and 7. NTFS is the file system of choice because it supports additional file attributes such as encryption using the Encrypting File System (EFS) and compression at both the file and folder levels. In addition, it incorporates two copies of the master file table for fault tolerance. Further, when used with current versions of Windows, NTFS supports granular file permissions based on the ownership of the file, or who created it. The NTFS file system structure is more complex compared with FAT16 or FAT32, and the file attributes are particularly usable when viewed in forensic software because each file has its own associated permissions allowing investigators to see the username account that last modified each file or folder. In this lab, you will add the C4Proj2.dd image to ProDiscover to view the NTFS file system attributes.

After completing this lab, you will be able to:

- Discuss the differences between NTFS and FAT16 or FAT32

- View the NTFS disk cluster structure

Materials Required

This lab requires the following:

- Windows Vista
- ProDiscover Basic
- C4Proj2.dd image

Estimated completion time: **15–20 minutes**

Activity

In this activity, you will add the C4Proj2.dd image to ProDiscover to view the additional NTFS file system attributes.

1. Double-click the **ProDiscover** icon on your desktop.

2. Click the **File** tab and click **New Project**.

3. In the New Project dialog box, type **C4Lab2** into the Project Number and Project File Name boxes. Enter **NTFS USB Device Image** in the Description area, and click **OK**.

4. Click the **Action** tab, and click **Add**; then in the submenu, click **Image File**.

5. In the Open dialog box, browse to the location of the **C4Proj2.dd** file in the InChap4 folder on the student data disk, click the file, and click **Open**.

6. Expand the **Images** icon located under Content View, and click the **C4Proj2.dd** image icon.

7. Note the files displayed in the root directory listing contain a different file system structure compared with the FAT32 image you analyzed earlier. Drag the bottom of the window down to view all the files listed at the bottom of the root directory. Notice that the deleted files are not listed in the root directory; only the remaining files are displayed. The two files listed in red support additional NTFS features. The $BadClus:$Bad file maintains a list of bad clusters encountered by the file system, and the $Secure:$SDS file contains the security attributes for EFS encryption. These are not supported in FAT16 or FAT32 file systems. Click the + symbol next to the image icon to expand it, and view the contents of the image.

8. Click the **Deleted Files** icon to display the deleted files located on this storage device.

9. Click the check box next to the first deleted file, and type **Deleted file** in the Add Comments dialog box. Click **OK**. Repeat this process for the other two deleted files.

10. Click the **$Extend** folder to display the folder structure that contains the NTFS permissions applied to parent and child files and folders. NTFS supports additional storage volume attributes that include compression, encryption, and support for disk quotas. These folders maintain the access control list and permissions available in NTFS-formatted partitions. FAT16 and FAT32 do not support these features, and their corresponding file system structures are much simpler in design.

11. Click the **Tools** tab, and click **Batch Calculate Hashing**. Click **Yes** in the ProDiscover dialog box to disregard the notification.

12. Click the **C4Proj2.dd image** icon. Click the **View** tab, and click **Gallery View** to display the graphic images (see Figure 4-4).

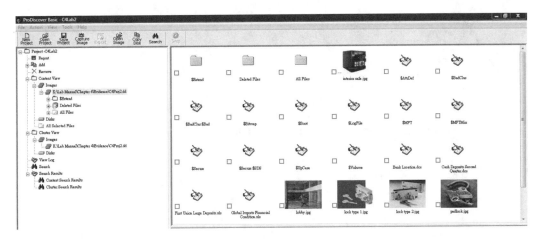

Figure 4-4   Graphic images in NTFS

Course Technology/Cengage Learning

13. Expand the + symbol next to the **Images** icon under the Cluster View, and click the **C4Proj2.dd** image icon to view the disk clusters and hex data representing the raw image displayed in the upper and lower windows, respectively. Note the NTFS file system signature listed in the lower window.

14. Click the **View** tab, and click **Report** to display the results of the investigation of this evidence.

15. Leave the report window open as you complete the follow lab questions. Click the **File** tab and click **Exit**. Select **No** in the ProDiscover dialog box to close ProDiscover.

Review Questions

1. What is the total number of clusters contained in this image?

   a. 512

   b. 120574

   c. 31487

   d. 251903

2. What is the total size of this storage device in kilobytes?

   a. 125951

   b. 512

   c. 251903

   d. 8

3. How many clusters did the deleted MS Word document occupy in the image?

   a. 11

   b. 5

   c. 6

   d. 8

4. What time was the bank.jpg file deleted?

   a. 22:16

   b. 12:59

   c. 1:39

   d. 10:56

5. How many sectors are contained in each cluster?

   a. 16

   b. 512

   c. 8

   d. 31487

Lab 4.3 Adding Forensic Evidence to Forensic Toolkit 1.81

Objectives

The AccessData Forensic Toolkit (FTK) contains many useful tools and is similar to ProDiscover; however, many forensics investigators find the former to be more user friendly. FTK places recovered files into separate file buckets based on the file category or status. The FTK interface allows investigators to view the file system structure, and it uses built-in file-type viewers to display each file in its native format without additional software. In this lab, you will add the C4Proj1.dd file to FTK and analyze the imaged evidence.

After completing this lab, you will be able to:

- Add evidence to FTK 1.81
- Bookmark files and create an HTML report using FTK 1.81

Materials Required

This lab requires the following:

- Windows Vista
- Forensic Toolkit (FTK) 1.81
- C4Proj1.dd image file

Estimated completion time: **20 minutes**

Activity

In this activity, you will add the C4Proj1.dd file to FTK 1.81.

1. Right-click the **FTK 1.81** icon on your desktop, and click **Run as administrator**. Click **Allow** in the User Account Control dialog box. If necessary, click **OK** in the CodeMeter.exe dialog box.

2. Click **OK** in the AccessData FTK dialog box describing the 5000 maximum limit in the trial version of this software. This error will appear each time you start FTK.

3. Select **Start a new case**, if necessary, in the AccessData FTK Startup dialog box, and click **OK**.

4. Enter your full name in the Investigator Name box, if necessary. Type **C4Lab3** in the Case Number and Case Name boxes located in the New Case dialog box. Click the **Browse** button, and navigate to the C:\Work\Labs\Cases\ folder, if necessary, to designate the Case Path. Click **Next** to continue.

5. Type your full name in the Examiner's Name box located in the FTK Report Wizard-Case Information dialog box, and click **Next** to continue.

6. Click **Next** four times to accept the default Case Log Options, the Processes to Perform, the Refine Case-Default, and the Refine Index-Default dialog boxes.

7. Click the **Add Evidence** button, and select **Acquired Image of Drive** if necessary in the Add Evidence to Case dialog box. Click **Continue**, and navigate to the **C4Proj1.dd** image file in the InChap4 folder on the student data disk, and then click **Open**. Type **C4Proj1** in the Evidence Identification Name/Number text box, and choose **Eastern Time with Daylight Saving** in the Local Evidence Time Zone. Click **OK**.

8. Click **Next** in the Case Summary dialog box, and click **Finish** in the New Case Setup is Now Complete dialog box. The Processing Files dialog box will appear; after the process has completed, you will see the FTK interface and the associated file buckets.

9. Locate the Documents bucket button under the File Category heading, and notice that five files are listed on the bucket button. Click the **Documents** bucket button to display the existing and deleted MS Word documents (see Figure 4-5). Move the scroll bar on the bottom of the lower window to display the file attributes, the logical and physical sizes, and their associated hash signatures.

10. Click the **Spreadsheets** bucket button to display the two existing and one deleted MS Excel files. Use the scroll bar to view all the file attributes, including their associated hash file signatures, if necessary.

11. Click the **Deleted Files** bucket button under the File Status column to view the deleted files and their associated file structures. Click the check box next to each deleted

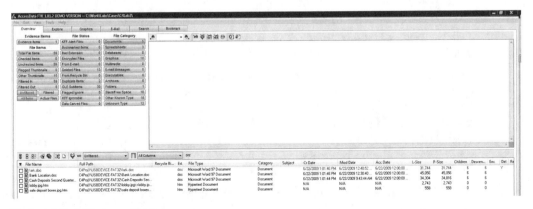

Figure 4-5 FTK document list

Course Technology/Cengage Learning

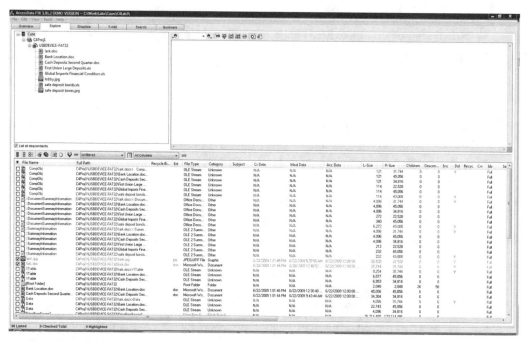

Figure 4-6   Explore tab

Course Technology/Cengage Learning

file icon, and right-click any deleted file, and click **Create Bookmark** from the shortcut menu. In the Create New Bookmark dialog box, type **Deleted files** in the Bookmark name text box, and click **All checked items** to add all the bookmarks. Check the **Include in report** box in Report options, and click **OK**. All the bookmarked file attributes will turn purple.

12. Click the **Explore** tab, and select the **List all descendants** check box to see the root directory listing of files and all the files listed in the lower windows. The bookmarked files will have the purple-colored attributes (see Figure 4-6).

13. Click the **Graphics** tab, and select the **List all descendants** check box to see the root directory listing of all the graphic image files in the lower window and the actual images in the top window. The bookmarked files will have the purple-colored attributes.

14. Click the **Bookmark** tab, and click the + symbol next to the **Deleted files** icon listed under Bookmarks in the upper window to see all the bookmarked files.

15. Click the **File** tab, and click **Report Wizard** on the drop-down list. Click **Next** to accept the default case information, and click **Next** in each dialog box to accept the Bookmarks-A, Bookmarks-B, Graphic Thumbnails, List by File Path, and List File Properties-A dialog boxes. Click **Next** in the FTK Report Wizard-Supplementary Files screen, and click **Finish** in the FTK Report Location dialog box. Click **Yes** in the Report Wizard dialog box to view the report. Click the **File Overview** link under Case Summary to see the File Overview (see Figure 4-7).

16. The FTK Case Report is an HTML-formatted web page that will be viewable in Internet Explorer or any browser. Click each of the links located on the left side of the window

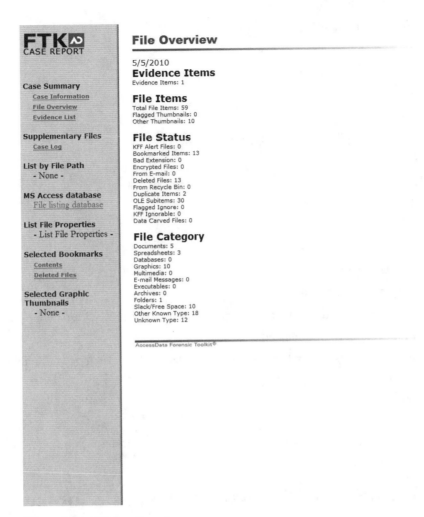

FTK ⌃⌄
CASE REPORT

Case Summary
    Case Information
    File Overview
    Evidence List

Supplementary Files
    Case Log

List by File Path
    - None -

MS Access database
    File listing database

List File Properties
    - List File Properties -

Selected Bookmarks
    Contents
    Deleted Files

**Selected Graphic
Thumbnails**
    - None -

File Overview

5/5/2010
Evidence Items
Evidence Items: 1

File Items
Total File Items: 59
Flagged Thumbnails: 0
Other Thumbnails: 10

File Status
KFF Alert Files: 0
Bookmarked Items: 13
Bad Extension: 0
Encrypted Files: 0
From E-mail: 0
Deleted Files: 13
From Recycle Bin: 0
Duplicate Items: 2
OLE Subitems: 30
Flagged Ignore: 0
KFF Ignorable: 0
Data Carved Files: 0

File Category
Documents: 5
Spreadsheets: 3
Databases: 0
Graphics: 10
Multimedia: 0
E-mail Messages: 0
Executables: 0
Archives: 0
Folders: 1
Slack/Free Space: 10
Other Known Type: 18
Unknown Type: 12

AccessData Forensic Toolkit®

Figure 4-7   FTK Case Report

Course Technology/Cengage Learning

to locate the report information. Leave this window open as you answer the review questions for this lab.

17. Close the FTK Case Report in your web browser. Click the **File** tab and click **Exit**; click **No** in the FTK Exit Backup Confirmation dialog box to close FTK.

Review Questions

1. In the File Overview link, how many Total File Items were recovered?

a. 10
 b. 59
c. 5
d. 13

2. What is the total number of deleted files?

    a. 59

    b. 5

    c. 13

    d. 10

3. How much Slack/Free Space is listed?

    a. 10

    b. 12

    c. 30

    d. 5

4. What is listed in the Case Log?

    a. all the deleted files and their associated attributes

    b. all the deleted file hash signatures

    c. a running log of all the work performed and the evidence with date and time stamps

    d. all the remaining files located and the evidence image

5. In the Deleted Files link, what is the physical size of the deleted graphics image file?

    a. 22,528

    b. 8,940

    c. 376

    d. 45

Lab 4.4 Viewing an NTFS Image in Forensic Toolkit 1.81

Objectives

The NTFS-formatted partition contains additional file structures to support enhanced file attributes such as encryption, compression, and file- and folder-level permissions. The FTK interface provides a detailed listing in the Explore tab, and the structure will be similar to the results obtained in Lab 4.2. In this lab, you will add the C4Proj2.dd image to FTK and process the recovered digital evidence.

After completing this lab, you will be able to:

- Add an NTFS-formatted image to FTK
- List the differences between FAT32 and NTFS
- Create an FTK report summary

Materials Required

This lab requires the following:

- Windows Vista

- Forensic Toolkit (FTK) 1.81
- C4Proj2.dd image

Estimated completion time: **20 minutes**

Activity

In this activity, you will add the C4Proj2.dd file to FTK 1.81.

1. Right-click the **FTK 1.81** icon on your desktop, and click **Run as administrator**. Click **Allow** in the User Account Control dialog box. If necessary, click **OK** in the CodeMeter.exe dialog box.

2. Click **OK** in the AccessData FTK dialog box describing the 5000 maximum limit in the trial version of this software. This error will appear each time you start FTK.

3. Click **Start a new case**, if necessary, in the AccessData FTK Startup dialog box, and click **OK**.

4. Type **C4Lab4** in the Case Number and Case Name boxes located in the New Case dialog box. Click **Next** to continue.

5. Click **Next** in the FTK Report Wizard-Case Information dialog box to continue.

6. Click **Next** four times to accept the default Case Log Options, the Processes to Perform, the Refine Case-Default, and the Refine Index-Default dialog boxes.

7. Click the **Add Evidence** button, and click **Acquired Image of Drive**, if necessary, in the Add Evidence to Case dialog box. Click **Continue**, and navigate to the **C4Proj2.dd** image file in the InChap4 folder located on the student data disk. Click the **C4Proj2.dd** file, and click **Open**. Type **C4Proj2** in the Evidence Identification Name/Number text box, and click **OK**.

8. Click **Next** in the Case Summary dialog box to start processing the evidence, and then click **Finish** to begin processing the evidence. The Processing Files dialog box will appear; after the process has completed, you will see the FTK interface and the associated file buckets.

9. Locate the Documents bucket button under the File Category heading, and notice that five files are listed on the bucket button. Click the **Documents** bucket button to display the existing and deleted MS Word documents. Move the scroll bar on the bottom of the lower window to display the file attributes, the logical and physical sizes, and their associated hash signatures.

10. Click the **Spreadsheets** bucket button to display the two existing and one deleted MS Excel files. Use the scroll bar to view all the file attributes, including their associated hash file signatures.

11. Click the **Deleted Files** bucket button located under the File Status column to view the deleted files and their associated file structures. Click the check box next to each deleted file icon, right-click any deleted file, and click **Create Bookmark** on the shortcut menu. In the Create New Bookmark dialog box, type **Deleted files** as the

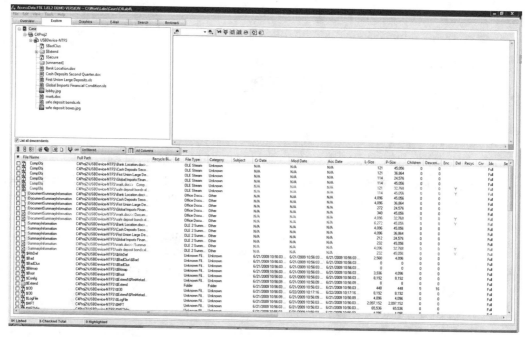

Figure 4-8   Explore tab in NTFS

Course Technology/Cengage Learning

Bookmark name, and click the `All checked items` button to add all the bookmarks. Check the `Include in report` box in Report options, and click `OK`. All the book-marked file attributes will turn purple.

12. Click the `Explore` tab, and select the `List all descendants` check box to see the root directory listing of files and all the files listed in the lower windows. The book-marked files will have the purple-colored attributes (see Figure 4-8). Note the additional $Extend and $Secure folders described in Lab 4.2 that are associated with NTFS-formatted partitions.

13. Click the `Graphics` tab, and select the `List all descendants` check box to see the root directory listing all the graphic image files in the lower window and the actual images in the top window. The bookmarked files will have the purple-colored attributes.

14. Click the `Bookmark` tab, and expand the `Deleted files` folder listed under Bookmarks in the upper window to see all the bookmarked files.

15. Click the `File` menu item, and click `Report Wizard` from the drop-down list. Click `Next` seven times to accept the default Case Information, Bookmarks-A , Bookmarks-B, Graphic Thumbnails, List by File Path, and List File Properties-A boxes, and the Supplementary Files screen. Click `Finish` in the Report Location dialog box. Click `Yes` in the Report Wizard dialog box to view the report.

16. View the FTK Case Report web page in Internet Explorer or any browser. Click each of the links to display the NTFS file report information. Leave this window open as you answer the review questions for this lab.

17. Close the FTK Case Report in your web browser. Click the `File` tab, and click `Exit` to close FTK.

Review Questions

1. What is the number of Total File Items recovered from the NTFS image?

    a. 30

    b. 13

    c. 91

    d. 10

2. What is the number of graphic images recovered from the NTFS image?

    a. 30

    b. 13

    c. 10

    d. 5

3. How many unknown file types are listed in the report?

    a. 45

    b. 18

    c. 1

    d. 30

4. What is the physical size of the deleted graphic image file?

    a. 22,528

    b. 24,576

    c. 31,744

    d. 43,008

5. What is the sector number for the deleted spreadsheet file?

    a. 118,464

    b. 14,808

    c. 14,818

    d. 118,544

PROCESSING CRIME AND INCIDENT SCENES

Labs included in this chapter

- Lab 5.1 Searching for Evidence in Forensic Toolkit
- Lab 5.2 Searching for E-mail Evidence Using Forensic Toolkit
- Lab 5.3 Searching for Keywords in Forensic Toolkit
- Lab 5.4 Creating a Final Report

Lab 5.1 Searching for Evidence in Forensic Toolkit

Objectives

When forensics investigators process evidence during an investigation involving computer-related crimes, they often need to create a bit-stream copy of the original evidence and analyze the forensically imaged copy. In Chapter 4, you learned about imaging techniques and how to verify the forensically duplicated image against the original disk using hash values. In this lab, you will add a drive image to Forensic Toolkit (FTK) and perform a cursory analysis of image contents to determine whether the image contains any potential evidence. Storage devices can contain millions of files and other objects that can take significant time to search. Forensics investigators need to quickly examine evidence and bookmark any suspicious files or information they encounter as they prepare their case.

After completing this lab, you will be able to:

- Locate documents and files in a storage device image
- Locate the hash files and file header information in MS Office documents

Materials Required

This lab requires the following:

- Windows Vista
- Forensic Toolkit (FTK) 1.81
- C5Proj1.dd

Estimated completion time: **10–15 minutes**

Activity

In this activity, you will add the C5Proj.dd image to FTK and begin your initial investigation of the evidence.

1. Right-click the **Forensic Toolkit 1.81** icon on your desktop, and click **Run as administrator**. Click **Allow** in the User Account Control dialog box. Click **OK** in the CodeMeter.exe dialog box, if necessary.

2. Click **OK** in the AccessData FTK dialog box describing the 5000 maximum limit in the trial version of this software. This error will appear each time you start FTK.

3. Select **Start a new case** in the AccessData FTK Startup dialog box, if necessary, and click **OK**.

4. Type **C5Lab1** in the Case Number and Case Name boxes located in the New Case dialog box. Verify the Case Path is listed as C:\Work\Labs\Cases\, and click **Next** to continue.

5. If necessary, type your full name in the Examiner's Name box located in the FTK Report Wizard-Case Information dialog box, and click **Next** to continue.

6. Click **Next** four times to accept the default Case Log Options, the Processes to Perform, the Refine Case-Default, and the Refine Index-Default dialog box.

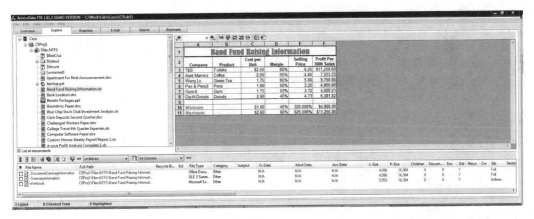

Figure 5-1 File viewer

Course Technology/Cengage Learning

7. Click the **Add Evidence** button and, if necessary, select **Acquired Image of Drive** in the Add Evidence to Case dialog box. Click **Continue**, and navigate to the **C5Proj1.dd** image file on the student data disk; click the file and click **Open**. Type **C5Proj1** in the Evidence Identification Name/Number text box. Click **OK**.

8. Click **Next** to start processing the evidence, and then click **Finish** in the New Case Setup is Now Complete dialog box. The Processing Files dialog box will appear. After the process has completed, you will see the FTK interface and the associated file buckets.

9. Click the **Explore** tab, and select the **List all descendants** check box. Notice all the files appear in the lower window. This box should always be checked to see all the parent and child files and folders.

10. Click the **C5Proj1** icon to view all the files and folders located in the root of the evidence storage device. Deleted files are represented by a red X in the icon next to the file name.

11. Click the deleted **Band Fund Raising Information.xls** file, and select the eyeglasses icon in the file toolbar to view the file in its native state or as it would appear in MS Excel (see Figure 5-1). Click several files listed in the root directory, and view them using the FTK file viewer.

12. Click the **Graphics** tab, and click in the check box marked **List all descendants**. All the graphic images recovered in the evidence are displayed in the top window. If you select any image in the top window, it will be displayed in the center window file viewer. Also note that as you view each image, the file name associated with the image will be highlighted in the lower window. Right click the **Pic_Safe1_Large.jpg** file in the bottom window, and click **File Properties** to view the file details.

13. The file name, the path to its location, and the file extension are listed for each file. Drag the scroll bar at the bottom of the lower window to the right to view the MD5 and SHA1 file hashes for the image, and adjust the column heading width for each hash to see the file signature. This file was attached to an e-mail message.

14. Click the **HEX** button in the toolbar to view the file header information displayed in hexadecimal notation. Locate the JFIF text in the right-middle window, and highlight it to view the hex file header for this file (see Figure 5-2). Every file type has a header that is associated with it.

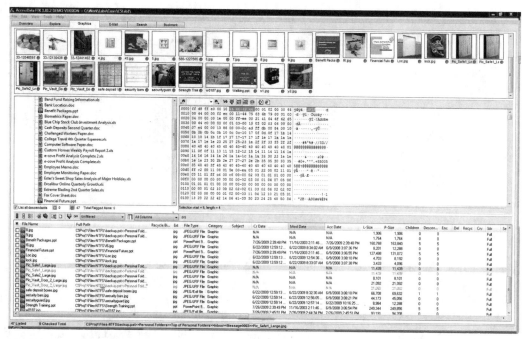

Figure 5-2 File header

Course Technology/Cengage Learning

15. Click the **Overview** tab, and select the **Deleted Files** bucket button. The total number of deleted items contained in the bucket are displayed. All the deleted files and their associated file structures are displayed in the lower window. Move the scroll bar to the right to display the file hashes for the deleted files.

16. Click the **Documents** bucket button, and notice that 21 documents are listed along with the file attributes and hash values for each file. Notice each document file has an associated physical and logical size as well as cluster and sector locations on the original storage device.

17. Click any MS Word document, and type **c** on the blue bolded line to search for the Cash Deposits Second Quarter document. The first letter search will move the file index to a matched file name. The file header indicating an MS Office document, d0 cf, is displayed in the first four hex bytes followed by the remaining document data in hex.

18. Answer the review questions using the FTK interface. When you are finished, click the **File** tab and select **Exit**. Click **No** in the FTK Exit Backup Confirmation dialog box.

Review Questions

1. What time was the Cash Deposits Second Quarter MS Word document last accessed?

   a. 9:43 AM

   b. 12:59 PM

   c. 2:37 PM

   d. 11:19 PM

2. Using the information contained in the Overview tab, how many spreadsheet files are located in this image?

    a. 376

    b. 24

    c. 47

    d. 21

3. How many deleted files were recovered in this image?

    a. 42

    b. 40

    c. 212

    d. 376

4. How many files are associated with e-mails?

    a. 42

    b. 40

    c. 47

    d. 212

5. How many e-mail messages were recovered in the image?

    a. 10

    b. 40

    c. 42

    d. 21

Lab 5.2 Searching for E-mail Evidence Using Forensic Toolkit

Objectives

E-mail evidence is undoubtedly one of the most import aspects of computer-related crimes because each e-mail message contains accurate time stamp information that cannot be altered without detection. When an e-mail message is sent, the sending computer places a header in the outgoing message that can be used to track the message from the source to the destination. In addition, time stamps are appended to the header as e-mail messages pass through each mail handler on their way to the recipient. Each e-mail server involved in the exchange of the message will have a record with the e-mail header information and its time stamp information. This allows investigators to verify the authenticity of the e-mail message and makes falsification of the e-mail message almost impossible without detection. In this lab, you will examine the e-mail records discovered in the previous lab.

After completing this lab, you will be able to:

- Identify the location of MS Outlook mailboxes

- Identify the file header information contained in an e-mail message

Materials Required

This lab requires the following:

- Windows Vista
- Forensic Toolkit (FTK) 1.81
- Completion of Lab 5.1 and the C5Proj1.ftk Case file

Estimated completion time: **15–20 minutes**

Activity

In this activity, you will look for e-mail evidence in the evidence you examined in Lab 5-1.

1. Right-click the **Forensic Toolkit 1.81** icon on your desktop, and select **Run as administrator**. Click **Allow** in the User Account Control dialog box. Click **OK** in the CodeMeter.exe dialog box, if necessary.

2. Click **OK** in the AccessData FTK dialog box describing the 5000 maximum limit in the trial version of this software. This error will appear each time you start FTK.

3. Select **Open an existing case** in the AccessData FTK Startup dialog box, and click **OK**.

4. FTK should remember the last default case location. If it does not, navigate to your C:\ Work\Labs\Cases folder, and locate and click the **C5Lab1**. Click the **C5Proj1.ftk** file, and click **Open** in the Open Case dialog box.

5. Click the **E-Mail** tab, and expand the **backup.pst** icon by clicking on the + symbol in the upper-left window. This file contains the MS Outlook database file taken from the suspect's hard drive.

6. Expand the **Personal Folders** and **Top of Personal Folders** folders to view the Outlook e-mail structure.

7. Each computer that has MS Outlook installed will have account folders for each e-mail account located on that computer. Select the **List all descendants** check box, and notice all the files that appear when this check box is selected. In most investigations, this check box should be checked.

8. The Top of Personal Folders folder contains child folders for Calendar, Contacts, Deleted Items, and Drafts, and the Inbox and Sent Items folders. Click the **Inbox** folder to view the inbound e-mail messages.

9. Click the **Message0003** e-mail message, and notice that it contains two attached graphic images; they are listed in the lower-right window. The actual e-mail message is displayed in the left window along with the sender's name and the time stamp details. The message attachments can be viewed by clicking each file attachment.

10. Use the scroll bar to view all the file attributes, and notice that each e-mail has an associated time stamp that is embedded into the e-mail header; they include the MD5 and SHA1 hash values for each message and its attachments. The e-mail header time stamps are almost impossible to alter without detection.

Figure 5-3   Sent e-mail messages

Course Technology/Cengage Learning

11. Click the **Sent Items** folder to view the sent messages. Each sent e-mail message contains the text time stamps and the embedded header time stamps. Use the scroll bar to view the hash values for the sent e-mail messages and their header information (see Figure 5-3).

12. Use the FTK interface to answer the review questions. Leave FTK open for the next lab.

Review Questions

1. How many e-mail messages are contained in the Inbox mailbox?

    a. 9

    b. 5

    c. 4

    d. 3

2. What is the subject of the third e-mail message?

    a. Microsoft Outlook Test Message

    b. Re: Safe

    c. Re: Profit Analysis

    d. no subject message

INDEX (handwritten)

3. Who sent the last e-mail message?

  a. mpeters24

  b. jdoe718

  c. jsmith954

  d. Outlook 2003 Team

Sent Items (handwritten)

4. What is the e-mail time of the second sent e-mail message?

  a. 9:05 PM

  b. 9:18 PM

  c. 9:38 PM

  d. 9:12 PM

5. How many graphic images were found in the Sent Items?

  a. 2

  b. 3

  c. 1

  d. 4

Lab 5.3 Searching for Keywords in Forensic Toolkit

Objectives

Forensics investigators need to search through files to locate keywords or phrases that may be contained in documents or other files. Often keywords may be useful in searching for evidence linked to a crime. In this lab, you will search for evidence linked to a bank robbery involving two people who may have communicated using e-mail. The bank robbers were familiar with the work schedule at the bank and were not detected as they compromised a number of safe deposit boxes.

After completing this lab, you will be able to:

- Perform keyword searches
- Refine a keyword search to find specific information

Materials Required

This lab requires the following:

- Windows XP or Vista
- Forensic Toolkit (FTK) 1.81
- Completion of Lab 5.2

Estimated completion time: **10–15 minutes**

Activity

In this activity, you will continue to work in FTK 1.81 software to search for keyword terms related to a possible bank robbery. This lab assumes that FTK is still open. If FTK has been closed after Lab 5.2, please complete Steps 1–4 in Lab 5.2 before beginning this lab.

1. Click the **Search** tab. Type **bank** in the Search Term text box on the Indexed Search tab, and click **Add.** In the Search Items window, the term **bank** has been added, and 18 hits in 11 files indicate a match for the term.

2. Type **vault** in the Search Term box, and notice the four hits displayed in the Indexed Words window. This tool can be used to search for terms before actually adding them to the case.

3. Click **Add** in the Search Items window; the two terms are displayed along with the cumulative results, which indicate the two words are found together in two files.

4. Click the blue **View Cumulative Results** button, and select **All files**, if necessary, in the Filter Search Hits dialog box. Click **OK**.

5. The two files that have both terms contained in them are located in the bottom window. Expand the + sign next to the 4 Hits in the upper-right window.

6. Click the first message to display the e-mail containing both **bank** and **vault** in the same document. The e-mail delivery time, sender name, recipient name, and e-mail message are displayed in the middle window (see Figure 5-4). Bookmark the file by selecting the check box next to the message.

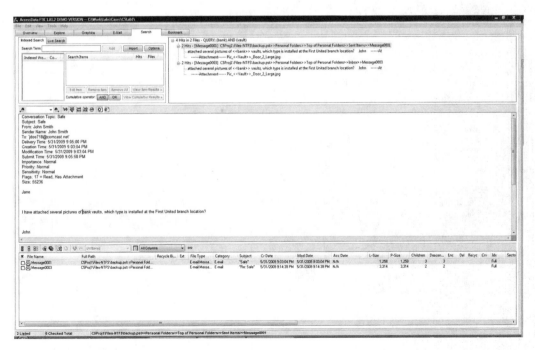

Figure 5-4   Live search hits

Course Technology/Cengage Learning

7. Click the second e-mail message to view its contents and attributes. Bookmark this file, and right-click the file and select **Create Bookmark**. In the Create New Bookmark dialog box, type **Email Evidence** and click **All checked items**. Confirm both messages appear under the File Name column, and check both the **Include in report** and the **Export files** boxes. Click **OK** to add the bookmarked files to the report.

8. Type **safe** in the Search Term text box, and click **Add**; confirm **safe** is now listed under the Search Items. Click **View Cumulative Results**, and click **OK** in the Filter Search Hits dialog box. The additional 34 hits found in the 10 files listed are now added to the file list, and each file can be viewed to search for additional evidence. Click the **34 Hits in 10 Files** list to see the locations where the word **safe** can be found.

9. Hold down the **Ctrl** key on the keyboard, and click each message to bookmark any file that may be related to a bank robbery case. When you have found all the e-mail messages, right-click the selected files and click **Create Bookmark**. In any bookmarked file, click **All highlighted items** in the Create New Bookmark dialog box. Type **Email Evidence** in the Bookmark Name text box, and click the **Include in report** and **Include parent of email attachments** check boxes. Click **OK** to add the files to the Email Evidence bookmarks.

10. The bank robbers forced the back door open to gain access to the bank. Search for "back door" to see whether this detail was planned. Type **back door** in the Search Term box, and look for the occurrence of both words in the Indexed Words. Because both do not appear together, try a cumulative search. Add the word **back** to the Search Items, and then add **door** to the Search Items. Notice that the two terms viewed in this manner return four hits in two files. Click **View Cumulative Results**. Click **OK**

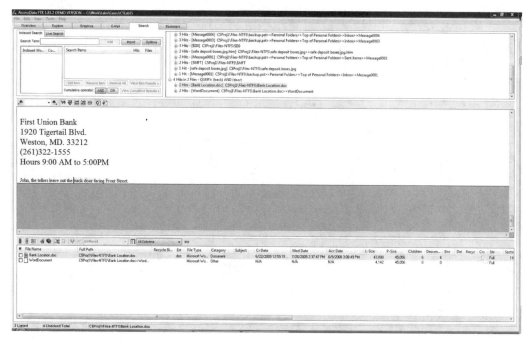

Figure 5-5 Cumulative search results

in the Filter Search Hits dialog box, and select **Bank Location** document listed in the bottom window to view the MS Word document (see Figure 5-5). Notice that the search engine found the MS Word document describing the back door along with other details of the crime.

11. Click the check box next to the Bank Location document, right-click the file, and click **Create Bookmark**. Type **Evidence** in the Bookmark name box. Click **All checked items**, and select both **Include in report** and **Export files** in the report options area. Click **OK**.

12. Click the **Graphics** tab, and click the check box next to the **List all descendants** box. You will see images that may be potential evidence. Select all images by holding the **Ctrl** button as you click each image.

13. Right-click any image you selected, and create a new bookmark called **Photo Evidence**. Verify both Report options check boxes are selected, and click **All highlighted items** to add the photos to the bookmarked items. Click **OK** to include the bookmarks in the final report.

14. Use the Bookmark tab or the Search tab to answer the review questions, and leave FTK open for the next lab.

Review Questions

1. Where did John Smith go to in his escape?

   a. New York

   b. Mexico

   c. Bora Bora

   d. Spain

2. Who was John's accomplice in the crime?

   a. Jane Doe

   b. Mark Peters

   c. John Smith

   d. Will Smith

3. Which exit do the tellers use to leave the bank?

   a. front door

   b. back door

   c. side door

   d. garage door

4. On what date was the Bank Location document created?

   a. 7/26/2009

   b. 6/9/2008

   c. 6/22/2009

   d. 7/1/2009

5. How many search queries are listed in the search details?

   a. 4

   b. 3  (You performed)

   c. 5

   d. 2

Lab 5.4 Creating a Final Report

Objectives

The final report includes bookmarks of evidence located and the scientific results obtained during the forensic investigation. It should contain a log file that highlights each tool applied to the evidence. The bookmarked files will also include the associated dates and time stamps. This report could be used by the forensics investigator to support his or her testimony in court or during a deposition. The report also serves to validate the chain of custody of the evidence, and it may be examined by the court during the trial. The report is crucial to the trial because it presents all the evidence obtained during the investigation in an easy-to-read format, and it can be used as physical evidence in place of the original evidence seized from the computer.

After completing this lab, you will be able to:

- Create a case report
- Describe the information contained in a case report

Materials Required

This lab requires the following:

- Windows Vista
- Forensic Toolkit (FTK) 1.81
- Completion of Lab 5.3

Estimated completion time: **10 minutes**

Activity

In this activity, you will create a report listing the evidence and all the forensic procedures performed during your investigation. This lab assumes that you have not closed Lab 5.3.

1. Click the **File** tab and select **Report Wizard**.

2. Type your full name in the Investigator's Name box, if necessary, and type **Bank Robbery** in the Comments area text box.

3. Click **Next** to continue, and in the FTK Reports Wizard-Bookmarks dialog box, select **Yes, include only bookmarks marked "Include in the report."** Click the check boxes next to **Include thumbnails of bookmarked graphics** and **Export full-size graphics and link them to the thumbnails**. If necessary, click **yes, export only files from bookmarks marked "Export to report"** (see Figure 5-6). Click **Next**.

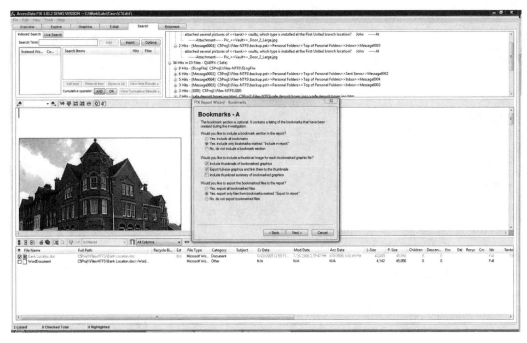

Figure 5-6   Bookmarks-A

Course Technology/Cengage Learning

4. Click **Next** in the Bookmarks-B dialog box, and click **Next** in the Graphic Thumbnails dialog box. Click **Next** in the List by File Path dialog box. Click **Next** in the List File Properties-A dialog box, and click **Next** in the Supplementary Files dialog box.

5. Click **Finish** in the Report Location dialog box to create the report.

6. Click **Yes** to view the report. The report will start Internet Explorer (or your default web browser), and the information will be organized by the links within the report.

7. Click the **Contents** link located under Bookmarks to display the three categories of bookmarked evidence located on the suspect's removable storage device. Click the **Email Evidence** list to display the e-mail messages along with their associated attachments.

8. Click the **Evidence** link to display the MS Word document information and a link to view the file.

9. Click the **Photo Evidence** link to view the graphic images found in the evidence and their associated file details, including the hash values.

10. Click **Case Log** to display the complete log file containing all the applied forensic tools and their results (see Figure 5-7). Note the time stamp information and search settings, including the keywords used in each query.

11. Answer the review questions using the information contained in the report. When you are finished answering the questions, close your Internet browser. In FTK, click the **File** tab and select **Exit**.

12. In the FTK Backup Confirmation dialog box, click **No** to exit FTK and close the evidence.

Figure 5-7   Case log

Course Technology/Cengage Learning

Review Questions

1. What was the total number of file items obtained from this evidence?

    a. 46

    b. 376   *Total File items*

    c. 152

    d. 107

2. What is the file system in use in this image?

    a. FAT16

    b. FAT32

    c. NTFS

    d. HFS+

3. How many file attachments are associated with Message0001?

    a. 1

    b. 3

    c. 2   *Sent Items*

    d. 4

4. What is the physical file size of the Bank Location document?

   a. 45,056

   b. 43,008

   c. 1,258

   d. 2,594

5. How many graphic images were bookmarked in the Photo Evidence?

   a. 10

   b. 15

   c. 5

   d. 12

WORKING WITH WINDOWS AND DOS SYSTEMS

Labs included in this chapter

- Lab 6.1 Examining the Windows XP SAM Hive
- Lab 6.2 Examining the Windows XP SYSTEM Hive
- Lab 6.3 Examining the Windows XP NTUSER.DAT Hive

Lab 6.1 Examining the Windows XP SAM Hive

Objectives

The Windows registry is the central repository that contains all the settings and data for the Windows environment. The registry is divided into five folders or hives, and they are located in the C:/Windows/System32/Config folder. Each registry hive provides specific data such as passwords, desktop settings, hardware and software configurations, and other valuable forensic information that may be useful during an investigation.

The Security Account Manager (SAM) contains information about the user accounts and their associated password hashes, as well as group definitions and domain associations. The actual passwords are not stored for security purposes, but many forensic tools can decrypt password hashes and allow investigators to gain access to password-protected areas of the computer. The SAM registry file stores information using Globally Unique IDs called GUIDs. GUIDs are 32 character hexadecimal tags that are stored as 128 bit integers and are used to identify operating system data such as usernames or hashed password locations. In this lab, you will exam a forensically secured Windows XP SAM registry file to locate usable forensic information.

After completing this lab, you will be able to:

- Identify the registry hive containing username and password hashes
- Add registry files to the AccessData Registry Viewer

Materials Required

This lab requires the following:

- Windows Vista
- AccessData Registry Viewer
- SAM file

> Estimated completion time: **15–20 minutes**

Activity

In this activity, you will examine the SAM Registry file to determine the user accounts located in the seized computer.

1. Double-click the **AccessData Registry Viewer** icon on your desktop, and click **Allow** in the User Account Control dialog box.

2. Click **OK** in the Codemeter.exe dialog box, if necessary, and click **OK** in the Registry Viewer dialog box (this message will appear each time the Registry Viewer is launched).

3. Click the **File** tab and select **Open**. Navigate to the InChap6 files, click the **SAM** file and select **Open**. Maximize the window to fill the entire desktop.

4. Click each + to expand the SAM, Domains, Account, and Users folders.

5. Click the first folder (**000001F4**), and locate the Key Properties folder in the lower-left window (see Figure 6-1). Drag the window boundaries to display all the data.

Figure 6-1 Administrator account information

Course Technology/Cengage Learning

6. The Key Properties window displays the information contained in each key folder. Click the scroll bar on the right side of the Key Properties to view all the attributes and to see whether this is an active account or a disabled account. The SID unique identifier field contains values that indicate the type of account and whether the account is a default account that is created automatically when the operation system is installed. The 500, 501, and 1000 values indicate default accounts that were automatically created.

7. Click the fifth folder (**000003EB**), and note that this created account was last used 5/14/2007. Also the SID value 1003 indicates that this is not a default account but rather a created account. The User Name is User, and the account has been accessed 24 times. Also note the date discrepancy between the Last Logon Time and the Last Password Change. This may indicate that the system time has been altered at least once.

8. Click the sixth folder (**000003EC**), and note that this account belongs to John Smith and the system time indicates that this account has also been modified to display a Last Logon Time as 5/15/2007 although the password was changed 5/31/2009. This account is also password protected.

9. Click the seventh folder (**000003EE**), and note that this account has not been used since it was created.

10. Expand the **Names** folder. Note the user account names, and click the jsmith account. The Last Written Time indicates that this account was accessed on 5/31/2009, whereas the last logon in Step 8 has a different date 2 years earlier. This should alert an investigator.

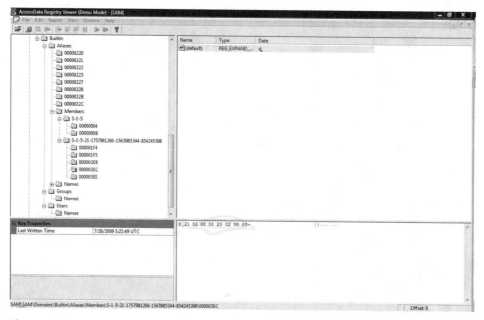

Figure 6-2   Account password hash

Course Technology/Cengage Learning

11. Expand the **Builtin** folder located under the Domains folder, and expand the **Members** folder to a folder that has a long number (the GUID). Windows uses GUID to hide actual names that might be used to locate critical information such as password hashes. Note the five folders that have the same number sequence as the Account folders. Click the **000003EC** folder (jsmith), and note the hex data in the lower-right windows, which represent the hashed password data (see Figure 6-2).

12. Leave the Registry Viewer application open while you answer the review questions.

13. Click the **File** tab and click **Exit**. Click **Yes** in the Registry Viewer dialog box to close the application.

Review Questions

1. How many user accounts are listed in the SAM hive?

    a. 3

    b. 2

    c. 7

    d. 6

2. How many user accounts are disabled?

    a. 2

    b. 7

    c. 1

    d. 3

3. How many Builtin accounts are disabled?

   a. 3

   b. 7

   c. 1

   d. 7

4. How many users have never logged into this computer?

   a. 5

   b. 3

   c. 1

   d. 7

5. How many user accounts require a password?

   a. 6

   b. 1

   c. 7

   d. 5

Lab 6.2 Examining the Windows XP SYSTEM Hive

Objectives

The SYSTEM registry hive contains drive letter designations for internal and external storage devices, the system name, and the configuration data for the system's hardware and software. This hive is very important because it can help identify on a specific computer any storage devices that may have been mounted into the operating system. The SYSTEM hive also contains information about when the Windows partition was created and activated. The Product ID Key (PID) is a unique identifier that can act as an electronic fingerprint uniquely identifying this Windows operating system. In this lab, you will add a Windows XP SYSTEM registry file to locate potential forensic information.

After completing this lab, you will be able to:

- Add the SYSTEM registration key to the Registry Viewer
- Look for useful forensic information in the SYSTEM registration key

Materials Required

This lab requires the following:

- Windows Vista
- AccessData Registry Viewer
- system file

Estimated completion time: **15 minutes**

Activity

In this activity, you will examine the SYSTEM registry file to identify the user accounts located on the seized computer.

1. Double-click the **AccessData Registry Viewer** icon on your desktop, and click **Allow** in the User Account Control dialog box.

2. Click **OK** in the Codemeter.exe dialog box, if necessary, and click **OK** in the No Dongle Found dialog box (this message will appear each time the Registry Viewer is launched).

3. Click the **File** tab, and select **Open** and navigate to the InChap6 files located on the student data disk. Click the **SYSTEM** file and click **Open**.

4. Click the + symbol next to the **ControlSet001** folder to expand it, and click the + symbol to expand the **Control** folder. Click the + symbol next to the **ComputerName** folder to expand it, and click the **ComputerName** child folder to display the name in the upper-right window.

5. Drag the scroll bar on the right side of the upper-left window down to view the TimeZoneInformation folder, and click it to display the computer's time zone bias. The time zone identification is critical because time stamp information is based on the time zone bias (see Figure 6-3).

6. Click the **Enum** folder, and expand it to view the subfolders. Select the **IDE** folder, and expand all the subfolders. This folder contains all the IDE storage devices, which include the CD-ROM and hard disk drive and their associated signatures.

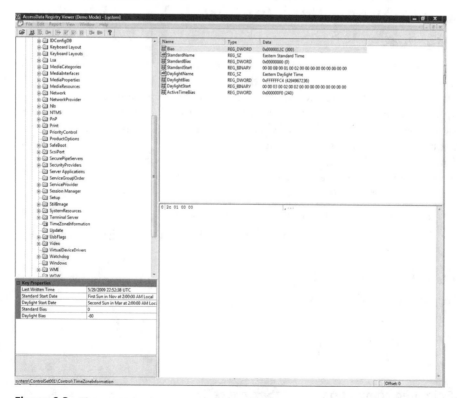

Figure 6-3   Time zone

Course Technology/Cengage Learning

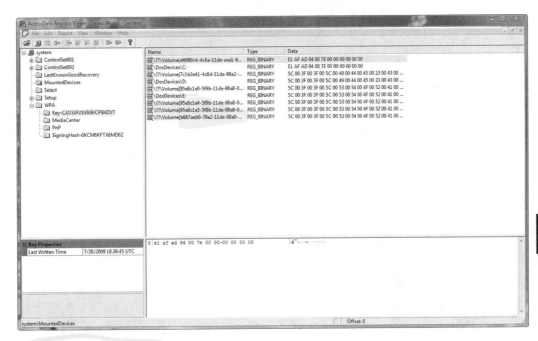

Figure 6-4   Mounted devices

Course Technology/Cengage Learning

7. Click the **USBSTOR** folder, and expand the folder to display all the USB storage devices that have been plugged into the computer. Note that each storage device has a unique serial number so that it can be identified. In addition, the Last Written Time is listed for each USB flash drive.

8. Click the **MountedDevices** folder. This folder lists every storage device that has been mounted in the operation system along with its associated drive letter (see Figure 6-4).

9. Expand the **WPA** folder. This folder contains the information on this unique copy of Windows. Select **system\WPA\Key-CJ27J3P2XV9J9JCPB4DVT**, and note the PID for this copy of Windows. Click the **SigningHash** folder, and look for the activation hash along with the Last Written Time. This information indicates that Windows was first installed and activated in 2009 and not 2007, as the user account key activity indicates.

10. Leave the Registry Viewer open as you answer the questions below. You may close the Registry Viewer if you are not continuing to the next lab.

Review Questions

1. What is the model of the hard drive used in this computer?

   a. Hitachi DK23AA-60

   b. CdRomHL-DT-ST_RW/DVD_GCC-4240N

   c. Dell_Memory_Key

   d. RemovableMedia

2. How many storage devices are connected to the IDE interface?

    a. 4

    b. 2

    c. 5

    d. 1

3. How many mounted devices have assigned drive letters?

    a. 2

    b. 3

    c. 1

    d. 4

4. What information is contained in the Enum folder?

    a. user account information

    b. password information

    c. file locations

    d. hardware and software values

5. What time (UTC) was this copy of Windows activated?

    a. 22:10:31

    b. 21:10:10

    c. 08:21:30

    d. 12:22:15

Lab 6.3 Examining the Windows XP NTUSER.DAT Hive

Objectives

The NTUSER.DAT registry hive contains user-specific information such as the desktop, Windows, software, and file settings. In addition, this registry hive stores the most recently used files and devices. The forensic information stored in this area can help investigators tie together documents, Internet searches, and recently used storage devices. The NTUSER.DAT file in Windows XP is located in the C:\Documents and Settings\Username folder, and there are separate folders and NTUSER.DAT files for each account holder in Windows. Many password decryption tools require both the NTUSER.DAT file and the SYSTEM registry hive to retrieve a user password. In this lab, you will add a Windows XP NTUSER.DAT registry file to locate potential forensic information.

After completing this lab, you will be able to:

- Add the NTUSER.DAT file to the Registry Viewer

- List several areas where user-specific forensic evidence may exist in the registry

Materials Required

This lab requires the following:

- Windows Vista
- AccessData Registry Viewer
- NTUSER.DAT file

Estimated completion time: **15 minutes**

Activity

In this activity, you will examine the forensically recovered Windows XP NTUSER.DAT file for forensic evidence.

1. Double-click the **AccessData Registry Viewer** icon on your desktop, and click **Allow** in the User Account Control dialog box.

2. Click **OK** in the Codemeter.exe dialog box, if necessary, and click **OK** in the No Dongle Found dialog box (this message will appear each time the Registry Viewer is launched).

3. Click the **File** tab, click **Open**, navigate to the InChap6 files, click the **NTUSER.DAT** file, and click **Open**. Maximize the Registry Viewer, if necessary, to view the entire display.

4. Click the **Edit** tab and click **Find**. In the Find dialog box, type **recent files** and press the **Enter** key. In the upper-right window, the two recently opened documents will be displayed along with the path to the files (see Figure 6-5).

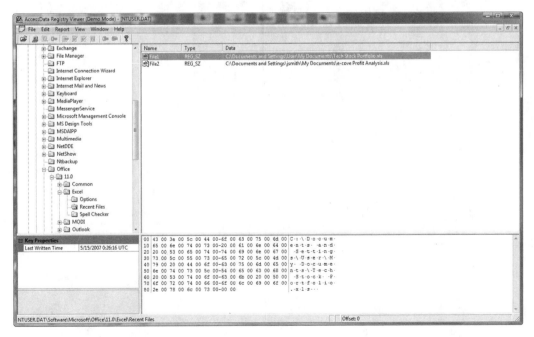

Figure 6-5   Recently opened files

Course Technology/Cengage Learning

5. Click the **Edit** tab and select **Find**. In the Find dialog box, type **jsmith** and click **Find Next** to search for the keys containing information about John Smith. The first search returns the username jsmith. Note that a manual search through each key would be very difficult and time consuming.

6. Press the **F3** key to search for the next reference to jsmith, which locates the Windows Logon User name.

7. Click the **Edit** tab and click **Find**. In the Find dialog, box type **email** and click **Find Next**. Click the **F3** function button to locate the e-mail account information for jsmith. Note the lower-right window displays the e-mail username in hex (see Figure 6-6). Use the arrow keys to scroll through the POP, SMTP, and password keys, and look for the text information in the hex area. The e-mail password is encrypted as displayed in hex (ASCII characters).

8. In the upper-left windows, click the drag scroll bar and drag it up to the top. Click the **NTUSER.DAT** computer icon. Click the **Edit** tab and select **Find**. In the Find dialog box, type **typedurls** and click **Find Next** to locate any URLs that were typed by jsmith. The only URL is listed in both the upper data window and the lower hex data area. Note the SearchUrl folder in the registry tree view in the upper-left window. This folder contains any URL that was searched.

9. Leave the Registry Viewer open as you answer the questions below. You may close the Registry Viewer when you are finished.

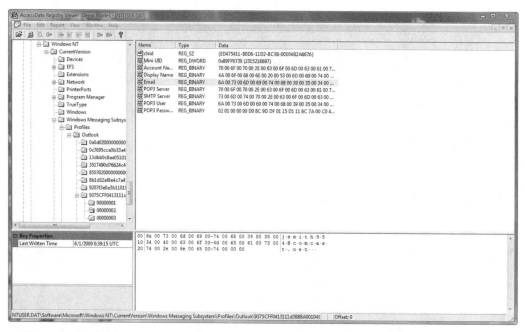

Figure 6-6   E-mail account

Course Technology/Cengage Learning

Review Questions

1. What type of files is listed in the recent files key?

    a. MS Word documents

    b. e-mail messages

    c. MS Excel files

    d. pictures

2. What is the POP3 Server name?

    a. POP.comcast.net

    b. SMTP.comcast.net

    c. jsmith.comcast.net

    d. sworth.comcast.net

3. How many web sites did jsmith search?

    a. 5

    b. 3

    c. 0

    d. 1

4. On what date did jsmith go to the Microsoft site?

    a. 6/1/2009

    b. 5/16/2007

    c. 5/31/2009

    d. 6/9/2009

5. Where is the Windows XP NTUSER.DAT file located?

    a. C:/Windows/System32/Config folder

    b. C:/Documents and Settings/User folder

    c. C:/SAM folder

    d. C:/SYSTEM folder

NTUSER . DAT \ SOFTWARE \

MICROSOFT \ Internet Explorer \

TYPE DULIS

CURRENT COMPUTER FORENSICS TOOLS

Labs included in this chapter

- Lab 7.1 Using FTK Imager to Analyze an Image
- Lab 7.2 Using the Forensic Toolkit to View Exported Evidence
- Lab 7.3 Advanced File Searching and Reporting

Lab 7.1 Using FTK Imager to Analyze an Image

Objectives

FTK Imager is typically used to create forensic copies of storage devices containing digital evidence. Typically an investigator would connect a suspected storage device such as a hard drive, solid-state storage device, or flash drive to a computer using a write-blocking device and capture the storage image in the form of an image file. This file may be scientifically analyzed using a number of different forensic tools available to the investigator. Although FTK Imager is primarily used to duplicate storage media, it also provides a quick way to view image files to locate possible evidence before it is processed by full-suite forensic tools, such as ProDiscover or AccessData's Forensic Toolkit (FTK). In this lab, you will add the image files of a seized hard drive that may contain evidence of a recent bank robbery involving safe deposit boxes and look for potential evidence that can be exported for further analysis.

After completing this lab, you will be able to:

- Add storage device image files to FTK Imager
- Use FTK Imager to export data files for further analysis

Materials Required

This lab requires the following:

- Windows Vista with MS Office 2003 or 2007 installed
- FTK Imager
- C7Proj01.zip file

Estimated completion time: **20–25 minutes**

Activity

In this activity, you will add the C7Proj01.001 evidence image to FTK Imager.

1. In your C:/Work/Labs folder, create a new folder named **Chapter 7**. Navigate to the InChap7 folder on your student data disk, right-click the **C7Proj01.zip** folder, and select **Extract All Files**. Click **Browse**, navigate to the Chapter 7 folder, click **OK**, and click **Extract** to extract the four image files to the C:/Work/Labs/Chapter 7 folder.

2. Double-click the **FTK Imager** icon on the Windows Desktop to launch FTK Imager.

3. Click the **File** tab, and select **Add Evidence Item**. In the Select dialog box, click **Image File** and then click **Next** to continue.

4. In the Select File dialog box, click **Browse**, navigate to the C:/Work/Labs/Chapter 7 folder, select the **C7Proj01.001** file, and click **Open**. In the Select File dialog box, click **Finish**. The Evidence Tree window displays the added evidence, and the Properties window displays the hard disk description and drive geometry.

5. In the Evidence Tree window, click the + symbol to expand the **C7Proj01.001**, **NONAME[NTFS]**, and **[root]** folders to reveal the root directory structure of the seized hard drive image.

6. Click the **NONAME[NTFS]** header, and locate the information listed in the File System Information. The Volume Serial Number identifies the physical hard drive. Right-click

the `C7Proj01.001` icon at the top of the evidence tree, and select **Verify Drive/ Image**. The MD5 and SHA1 image hashes will be displayed in the Drive/Image Verify Results dialog box. Click **close** in the Drive/Image Verify Results dialog box.

7. Click the **[root]** folder. In the Properties window, the Date Accessed information describes the last time and date this hard drive was accessed by a logged-in user (see Figure 7-1).

8. Navigate down in the Evidence Tree window, and click the + symbol to expand the **Documents and Settings** folder to view the user accounts on this hard drive. Click the **jsmith** folder to locate the last time jsmith logged into the computer in the Date Accessed area located in the Properties window. Click the **My Documents** folder under the **jsmith** folder to see all the user's documents. A file icon with a key symbol indicates a password-encrypted file.

9. Scroll down to the first NTFS Access Control Entry in the Properties window, and locate the system identifier (SID) value. Drag the right and top borders of the Properties

Figure 7-1   The root attributes

Course Technology/Cengage Learning

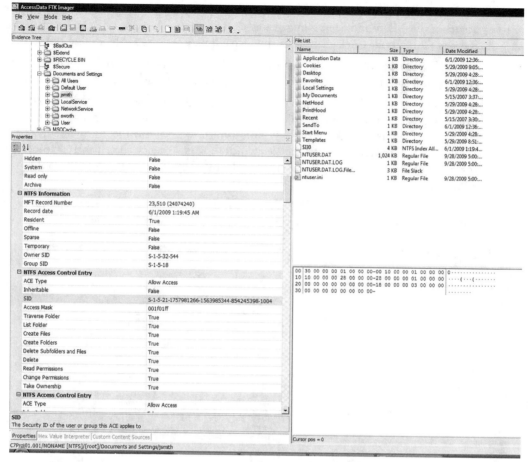

Figure 7-2 The jsmith SID

Course Technology/Cengage Learning

window to see all the details, if necessary. The last four numbers (1004) are jsmiths's unique SID (see Figure 7-2).

10. The jsmith user account files are displayed in the left File List window. Note the NTUSER.DAT registry file. This file is exported to recover the user password. Click the **My Documents** folder to view jsmith's existing files. Click on the Bank Locations. doc file, and you should see the document in MS Office 2003 or 2007. Click the **HEX Eyeglass** icon, and look for the first 2 bytes (d0 cf), which represent the file header signature.

11. Right-click the **jsmith** folder, and select **Export Files**. In the Browse for Folder dialog box, navigate to the C:/Word/Labs/Evidence folder. Click **Make New Folder**, type **C7Proj01**, and click **OK**. In the Export Results dialog box, click **OK**. Click the **sworth** folder, and select **Export Files**. In the Browse for Folder dialog box, navigate to the C:/Word/Labs/Evidence/C7Proj01 folder, and click **OK**. Click **OK** in the Export Results dialog box. The exported file will be used in the next lab exercise.

12. Locate the RECYCLER folder under the Program Files folder, and click the + symbol to expand it and reveal the three user account recycle bins. Each globally unique ID (GUID) contains the SID, which identifies the user accounts. SIDs 1003 and 1004 belong to jsmith and sworth, respectively. Select the **1006 GUID**, and look for any deleted MS Office files in the Recycle Bin. Export any MS Office files found to the C:/Work/Labs/ Evidence/C7Proj01 folder you created in Step 11.

13. Leave the FTK Imager application open as you answer the review questions for this lab.

14. Click the **File** tab, and select **Exit** to close the FTK Imager program.

Review Questions

1. What is the file system used on this hard disk image?

    a. FAT

    b. FAT32

    c. NTFS

    d. HFS+

2. How many encrypted files were located in jsmith's My Documents folder?

    a. 1

    b. 4

    c. 6

    d. 2

3. What is jsmith's unique SID?

    a. 513

    b. 1004

    c. 1003

    d. 501

4. On what date did sworth last delete files?

    a. 9/15/2007

    b. 5/15/2007

    c. 6/1/2009

    d. 9/28/2009

5. What is the hard disk Volume Serial Number?

    a. 1C17-C723

    b. S-1-3-0

    c. S-1-5-32-544

    d. S-1-5-18

7

Lab 7.2 Using the Forensic Toolkit to View Exported Evidence

Objectives

AccessData's FTK is a suite of tools that can be used independently or collectively to extensively examine storage devices for any digital evidence. Forensic tools must be capable of searching literally millions of files on large hard drive partitions. Files that are suspicious are saved for later examination, whereas files that are irrelevant are discarded. Without this capability, it could take significantly longer to process digital evidence. In Lab 7.1, you added the hard disk image to FTK Imager to locate potential evidence. During the investigation, several files were exported to your work folder for further analysis. In this lab, you will import the exported files and look at each file to see whether it contains potential evidence.

After completing this lab, you will be able to:

- Add files contained in a folder to FTK

- Bookmark individual files that contain evidentiary data

Materials Required

This lab requires the following:

- Windows Vista

- Forensic Toolkit (FTK) 1.81

- The exported files from Lab 7.1

Estimated completion time: **20–25 minutes**

Activity

In this activity, you will import the exported files into FTK to look for potential evidence.

1. Right-click the **Forensic Toolkit 1.81** icon on your desktop, and click **Run as administrator**.

2. Click **Allow** in the User Account dialog box. Click **OK** in the CodeMeter.exe dialog box, if necessary.

3. Click **OK** in the AccessData FTK dialog box describing the 5000 maximum limit in the trial version of this software. This error will appear each time you start FTK.

4. Select **Start a new case** in the AccessData FTK Startup dialog box, if necessary, and click **OK**.

5. Type **C7Proj02** in both the Case Number and Case Name text boxes, and click **Next** six times until the Add Evidence to Case dialog box appears.

6. In the Add Evidence to Case dialog box, click **Add Evidence**. In the Add Evidence to Case dialog box, select **Contents of a Folder**, and click **Continue**. In the Browse for Folder dialog box, navigate to the C:/Work/Labs/Evidence/C7Proj01 folder where you exported the files from Lab 7.1. Click **OK**, and in the Evidence Information dialog box, click **OK**.

7. Click **Next** in the Add Evidence to Case dialog box, and click **Finish** in the Case Summary dialog box. The evidence will be examined and indexed by FTK to sort the files into the FTK buckets.

8. Click the **Documents** bucket button under the File Category column to examine the recovered MS Word documents. Click the **Eyeglass** icon (native file viewer) if necessary, and select each document (.doc) file in the lower file window. You should see the document content in the upper viewer window; use the scroll bar, if necessary, to view the entire document (see Figure 7-3). Right-click the **Bank Location.doc** document, and select **Create Bookmark**. In the Create New Bookmark dialog box, type **Document Evidence**, and click **OK** to bookmark this file.

9. Click the **Spreadsheets** bucket button to examine the recovered MS Excel files. Click the **First Union Large Deposits.xls** file to display the file in the viewer. Drag the bottom scroll bar to see the physical and logical locations of the files on the hard drive. Notice the file header and the hash information for each file. Hold down the **Control** button, and select the **Global Imports Financial Condition.xls** file, right-click the file, and select **Create Bookmark**. In the Create New Bookmark dialog box, type **Document Evidence** in the Bookmark name box, verify that the **All highlighted items** button is selected, and click **OK** to bookmark these files (see Figure 7-4).

10. Click the **Graphics** tab, and check the **List all descendants** box. Notice that no images are displayed in the viewer until the check box is selected. Click each image in the upper window, and note the corresponding file attributes will be highlighted in the bottom window. Each recovered graphics image has an associated hash and file

Figure 7-3 Recovered document

Course Technology/Cengage Learning

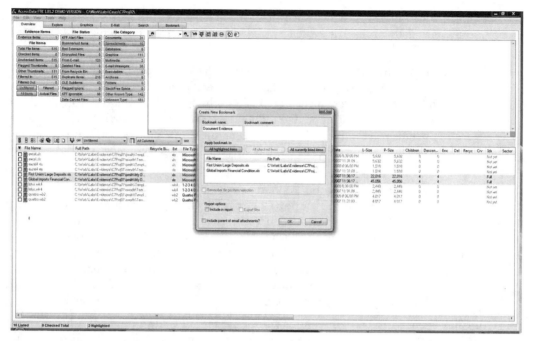

Figure 7-4 Bookmarking files

Course Technology/Cengage Learning

header value, which can be seen in the lower window using the scroll bar. In the upper window, click each image related to banks, locks, or security, and click the check box next to each file detail in the lower window to bookmark each one. Right-click on any checked file, and select **Create Bookmark**. In the Create New Bookmark dialog box, type **Image Evidence** in the Bookmark name box, click the **All checked items**, and click **OK**.

11. Click the **Hex Eyeglass** icon, and select any file listed in the lower window. Type the letter **l**, and notice that the lobby file is selected. In the middle hex window, locate the EXIF camera information describing the camera that captured the image (see Figure 7-5).

12. Click the **Overview** tab, and select the **Total File Items** bucket button. Scroll through the file list using the scroll bar, and notice all the bookmarked files that have their associated attributes listed in a lavender font. These files are included in the bookmark section.

13. Click the **Bookmark** tab to see the Document Evidence and Image Evidence listed in the tree structure, and click each bookmark to verify the files you added in Steps 8–11. Notice the bookmarked files are grouped by their descriptions.

14. Leave FTK open while you answer the review questions below.

15. Close the FTK application. Click **No** in the FTK Exit Backup Confirmation dialog box. FTK will close.

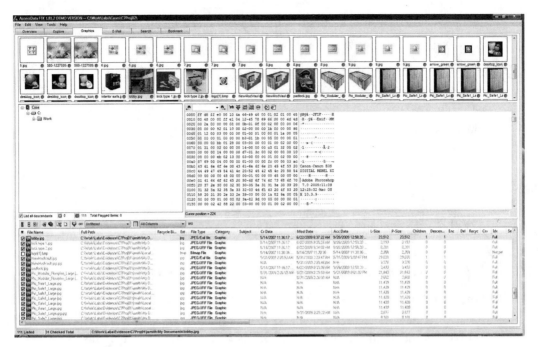

Figure 7-5 Recovered graphics

Course Technology/Cengage Learning

Review Questions

1. How many documents were filtered into the Documents bucket?

    a. 31

    b. 24

    c. 10

    d. 133

2. How many files have been bookmarked for later examination?

    a. 9

    b. 33

    c. 10

    d. 133

3. What file header describes images?

    a. DOCF

    b. JPGF

    c. JFIF

    d. DCFF

4. Whose name is mentioned in the Bank Location document?

   a. Jane

   b. John

   c. Steve

   d. Sally

5. When was the lobby file last accessed?

   a. 5/14/2007

   b. 6/22/2009

   c. 5/31/2009

   d. 9/28/2009

Lab 7.3 Advanced File Searching and Reporting

Objectives

FTK includes powerful search tools that can be used to search for keywords or combinations of keywords occurring in the same file using cumulative results. This can significantly decrease the search time and allow the investigator to focus on relevant evidence and discard useless information not pertinent to the investigation. After the forensic examination, investigators are required to complete reports indicating their findings for use by the court during the trial. The report also serves to document all the scientific methods used by the forensics investigator using the software tools. During the testimony, the investigator can refer back to the report to justify methods used in obtaining results.

After completing this lab, you will be able to:

- Use single and compound terms to search for potential evidence in the image file
- Create detailed reports highlighting the methods used along with the investigatory results

Materials Required

This lab requires the following:

- Windows Vista
- Forensic Toolkit (FTK) 1.81
- The C7Proj02.ftk file (completed in Lab 7.2)

Estimated completion time: **30–40 minutes**

Activity

In this activity, you will search for the occurrence of names in potential evidence and generate an investigatory report summarizing your results.

1. Right-click the **Forensic Toolkit 1.81** icon on your desktop, and click **Run as administrator.**

2. Click **Allow** in the User Account dialog box. Click **OK** in the CodeMeter.exe dialog box, if necessary. Click **OK** in the AccessData FTK dialog box describing the 5000 maximum limit in the trial version of this software. This error will appear each time you start FTK.

3. In the AccessData FTK Startup dialog box, select **Open an existing case**, and click **OK**. In the Open Case dialog box, select the **C7Proj02.ftk** file located on your C:\Work\Labs\Cases\C7Proj02 folder, and click **Open**. The backed-up case is now loaded into FTK.

4. Click the **Search** tab, and type **bank** into the Search Term text box. Notice that the Indexed Words window indicates that the word **bank** occurs in 46 times. Click the **Add** button, and in the Search Items window you will see 46 hits in 30 files. Click the **bank** search item, click **View Item Results**, and click **OK** in the Filter Search Hits to display the files that contain the word **bank**. Click the + symbol next to the 46 Hits in 30 Files list in the upper-right window to see the listed locations.

5. Type **john** in the search term box, and notice that there are 131 instances of John's name in the exported evidence. Click the **Add** button, and in the Search Items window you will now see 128 hits in 21 files in the Cumulative Results. The Cumulative Results displays files that contain the words **bank** and **john** in the same documents; these files may provide clues as to John's involvement with the crime. Click the **View Cumulative Results** button, select **All files** in the Filter Search Hits dialog box, and click **OK** to examine the hit results. Click the + symbol next to the 128 Hits in 21 Files list, scroll down to the first 3 Hits - [Bank Location.doc], and click in the link to display the document that contains both words highlighted in yellow (see Figure 7-6).

6. In one of the files, the name Jane appears. To see whether Jane and John are involved, perform a cumulative search of both names. Type **John**, and add his name to the Search Items followed by **Jane**. Notice that the Cumulative Results of both names produce

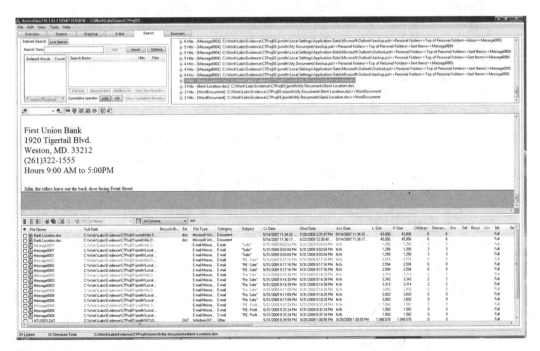

Figure 7-6 Cumulative Results search

Course Technology/Cengage Learning

126 hits in 18 files. Click the **View Cumulative Results** button, select **All files** in the Filter Search Hits dialog box, and click **OK** to examine the hit results. Click the + symbol next to 126 Hits in 18 Files – Query: (john) AND (jane), click the first hit [Message0002], and notice the incriminating e-mail message indicating that both John and Jane are involved in the crime. As you examine the remaining five hits, you will see an exchange of e-mail messages between John and Jane.

7. It is now time to create a report highlighting the investigation methods used in FTK and documenting the results. Click the **File** tab and select **Report Wizard**. In the FTK Report Wizard – Case Information dialog box, click **Next**. In the FTK Report Wizard – Bookmarks dialog box, select the **Yes, include all bookmarks** and **Yes, export all bookmarked files** radio buttons, and click **Next**.

8. Click **Next** in the Bookmarks – B dialog box, and in the Graphic Thumbnails dialog box, select the **Yes, include only graphics flagged green in the Graphics View** radio button, if necessary. Select the **6 per row** radio button, and click **Next**.

9. Accept the default settings in the List by File Path dialog box, and click **Next** to continue. In the List File Properties – A and the Supplementary Files dialog boxes, click **Next**.

10. In the Report Location dialog box, verify that the Report folder displays C:\Work\Labs\Cases\C7Proj02\Report\ as the path, and check the **Export all files using actual filenames** box. Click **Finish** to complete the report wizard, and select **Yes** in the Report Wizard to view the report (see Figure 7-7).

11. The FTK report is an HTML-based file that is viewed in an Internet browser such as Internet Explorer. The links on the left side of the window provide the path to the case log file that documents the forensic investigation process, including all the steps taken and any search items. When you click the link, you will see the time and date stamps for each process used. This log file maintains the chain of custody, and it is recognized as official evidence because it is computer generated. Click the **Document Evidence** link to display the two MS Excel files along with their associated time stamps, file headers, and hashes.

12. Click the **Image Evidence** link to display each bookmarked image along with their associated time stamps, file headers, and hashes.

13. Click the **Case Log** link under **Supplementary Files** to view the log file indicating all the processes performed on the evidence.

14. Leave both the report window and FTK open as you answer the reviews questions for this lab.

15. Click the **File** tab, select **Exit**, and click **No** in the FTK Exit Backup Confirmation dialog box to close FTK. Close the FTK Case Report.

Review Questions

1. How many graphics files were recovered in the evidence?

    a. 10

    b. 31

    c. 111

    d. 16

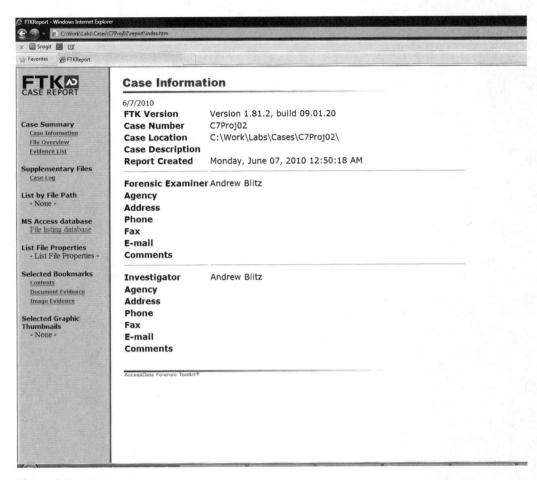

Figure 7-7   FTK Case Report

Course Technology/Cengage Learning

2. In the cumulative results for John and Jane, who had access to the bank at night?

    a. Jane

    b. John

    c. Steve

    d. Sally

3. What did John send via e-mail to Jane to look at?

    a. addresses of banks

    b. bank doors

    c. bank vaults

    d. armored cars

4. Using the FTK report, what time was the Bank Location document created?

   a. 11:36:17

   b. 12:31:34

   c. 10:56:19

   d. 12:12:34

5. Using the FTK report, what is the physical size of the lobby image file?

   a. 3,193

   b. 23,512

   c. 8,201

   d. 29,030

CHAPTER EIGHT

MACINTOSH AND LINUX BOOT PROCESSES AND FILE SYSTEMS

Labs included in this chapter

- Lab 8.1 Using Forensic Tools to Examine an OS X Macintosh Image
- Lab 8.2 Using Forensic Tools to Examine an OS 9 Macintosh Image
- Lab 8.3 Using FTK Imager and the Forensic Toolkit to Process a Linux Image

Lab 8.1 Using Forensic Tools to Examine an OS X Macintosh Image

Objectives

We have seen previously that FTK Imager can process Macintosh, Linux, UNIX, and Windows file systems. Although it is designed to facilitate the imaging process, it can provide useful information and allow evidence found on an HFS+ OS X partition to be exported into Forensic Toolkit (FTK) 1.81 for forensic analysis. This process may be useful to forensics investigators requiring analysis of HFS+ partitions using Windows-based tools that may not directly support Macintosh file systems. The HFS+ file system is an improved version of the HFS file system supporting large disk sizes used in today's computers. The HFS+ or Mac OS Extended file system was introduced in the release of OS X 10.3, and it is used in the current 10.6 version known as Snow Leopard. In this lab, you will extract the OS X image file from the lab book compressed files and export the useful user information to be added to the FTK for evidentiary processing.

After completing this lab, you will be able to:

- Process an OS X disk image and look for preliminary evidence
- Export folders created in OS X and use FTK to search for evidence

Materials Required

This lab requires the following:

- Windows Vista with Adobe Reader installed
- OSX.zip
- FTK Imager
- Forensic Toolkit (FTK) 1.81
- Hard drive with 20 GB of free space

Estimated completion time: **15–20 minutes**

Activity

In this activity, you will extract the OS X image from the InChap08 folder on the student data disk and import the image into FTK Imager to export possible forensic data into FTK.

1. Create a **Chapter 8** folder in your C:\Work\Labs folder. Navigate to the InChap8 folder on the student data disk, right-click the **OSX.zip** file, and click **Extract All**. Click **Browse**, navigate to the C:\Work\Labs\Chapter 8 folder, and click **OK** in the Select a Destination dialog box. Click **Extract** in the Extract Compressed (Zipped) folders to extract the OS X image into the Chapter 8 folder.

2. Double-click the **FTK Imager** icon located on your desktop. When FTK Imager has finished loading, click the **File** tab and select the **Add Evidence Image** item.

3. Select the **Image File** radio button in the Select Source dialog box, and click **Next**.

4. Click the **Browse** button, navigate to the extracted OS X folder, select the **GCFI-OSX.001** image file, and click **Open** (see Figure 8-1). Click **Finish** in the Select File dialog box.

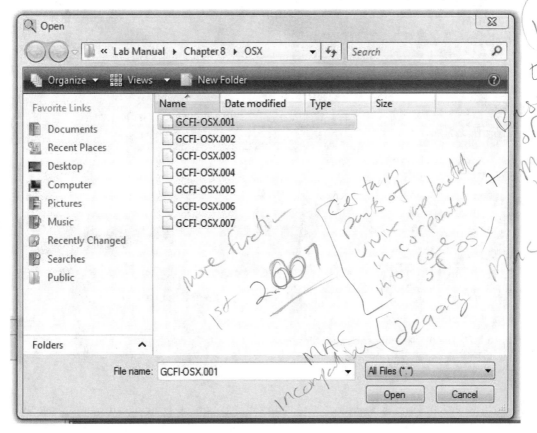

Figure 8-1 Select the OS X image file

Course Technology/Cengage Learning

5. In the upper-left Evidence Tree window, click the **+** symbols to expand the GCFI-OSX.001, Shu Systems [HFS+], and Shu Systems folders to display the list of directories located in the OS X root. Examine the folder structure, and note the differences between OS X and Windows.

6. Expand the **Users** folder, and note the user account listed. OS X creates a folder for each user and also creates a Shared folder to allow users to share files. Click the **+** symbol to expand the jimshu folder, and click the **Documents** folder to view jimshu's documents.

7. Locate the **02 Bike Helmet Use.pdf** file, and select the unlabeled **Eyeglass** icon on the tool bar in FTK Imager to view the .pdf file. Additional pages in the .pdf file can be viewed by clicking the blue page select arrows next to the page number box (see Figure 8-2).

8. The file properties—including the date/time information, logical file location and size, user ID, and UNIX file permissions—are located in the lower-left Properties window.

9. Right-click the **jimshu** folder, and select **Export Files**. In the Browse for Folder dialog box, locate the C:\Work\Labs\Evidence folder, and click **OK** to export the files. Click **Close** in the Export Results dialog box. Click the **File** tab, and click **Exit** to close the FTK Imager application.

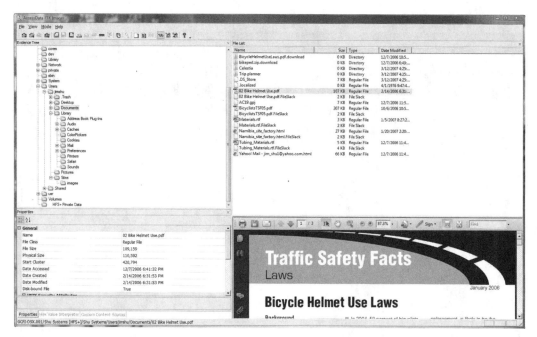

Figure 8-2   The 02 Bike Helmet Use.pdf file

Course Technology/Cengage Learning

10. Right-click the **Forensic Toolkit 1.81** icon on your desktop, and click **Run as administrator**.

11. Click **Allow** in the User Account dialog box. Click **OK** in the CodeMeter.exe dialog box, if necessary.

12. Click **OK** in the AccessData FTK dialog box describing the 5000 maximum limit in the trial version of this software. This error will appear each time you start FTK.

13. Select **Start a new case** in the AccessData FTK Startup dialog box, if necessary, and click **OK**. Type **C8Proj1** in both the Case Number and Case Name text boxes, and click **Next** six times until the Add Evidence to Case dialog box appears.

14. Click **Add Evidence**, select the **Contents of a Folder** radio button, and click **Continue** in the Add Evidence to Case dialog box. In the Browse for Folder dialog box, navigate to the jimshu folder in the C:\Work\Labs\Evidence, click it, and click **OK**. Click **OK** in the Evidence Information dialog box. Click **Next** in the Add Evidence to Case dialog box, and click **Finish** in the Case Summary dialog box to begin processing the evidence. This process may take a few minutes to complete.

15. Click the **Documents** bucket button, and select the first **Eyeglass** icon if necessary in the tool bar to examine the documents extracted from the OS X image (see Figure 8-3).

16. Leave the FTK 1.81 program open as you answer the review questions for this lab.

17. Click the **File** tab and click **Exit**. Click **No** in the FTK Exit Backup Confirmation dialog box to close the FTK program.

Figure 8-3 jimshu documents

Course Technology/Cengage Learning

Review Questions

1. How many document files were found in the jimshu account folder?

   a. 1417

   b. 65

   c. 95

   d. 1271

2. What is the subject of the incoming message from Jim Shu? (*Hint:* Use the E-mail tab.)

   a. Sebastian

   b. Jim Shu

   c. superiorbicycles

   d. Free tools

3. How many viewable picture files are attached to e-mails?

   a. 1

   b. 3

   c. 2

   d. 5

4. What is the name of the bad extension file?

   a. AC19.gpj

   b. apache_pb.gif

   c. PICT0032

   d. PICT0059

5. Who sent the 20th e-mail message to Jim Shu?

   a. Martha Dax

   b. Sebastian Mwangonde

   c. Nau Tjeriko

   d. Bart Johnson

Lab 8.2 Using Forensic Tools to Examine an OS 9 Macintosh Image

Objectives

The Macintosh OS 9 operating system is also known as Apple's "Classic" Mac OS. This operating system was introduced in 1999, and it lacked many of the modern features found in today's file systems, such as protected memory and preemptive multitasking. In 2002, Apple officially discontinued OS 9 and developed the current line of OS X operating systems. Forensics investigators may still encounter OS 9 images on older Apple computers still in use. Although the FTK 1.81 does not directly support Macintosh file systems, investigators can extract potential evidence into FTK using FTK Imager. In this lab, you will use the FTK Imager to extract the user account information contained in the OS 9 image files and search for potential evidence.

After completing this lab, you will be able to:

- Extract user account information from an OS 9 image
- Import extracted account information into FTK for processing

Materials Required

This lab requires the following:

- GCFI-OS9.zip file
- FTK Imager
- Forensic Toolkit (FTK) 1.81
- Windows Vista

Estimated completion time: **15–20 minutes**

Activity

In this activity, you will extract the OS 9 image and import it into FTK Imager to process evidence.

1. Create an OS 9 folder in the C:\Work\Labs\Chapter 8 folder. Navigate to the InChap8 folder on the student data disk, right-click the **GCFI-OS9.zip** file, and click **Extract All**. Click **Browse** in the Extract Compressed (Zipped) Folders dialog box, navigate to the C:\Work\Labs\Chapter 8\OS9 folder, and click **Extract** to upzip the files to the folder.

2. Double-click the **FTK Imager** icon located on your desktop. When FTK Imager has finished loading, click the **File** tab, and select **Add Evidence Item**.

3. Select the **Image File** radio button in the Select Source dialog box, and click **Next**.

4. Click the **Browse** button, and navigate to the C:\Work\Labs\Chapter 8\OS9 folder, select the **GCFI-OS9.001** image, and click **Open** (see Figure 8-4). Click **Finish** in the Select File dialog box.

5. In the upper-left Evidence Tree window, click the + symbols to expand the GCFI-OS9.001, the untitled [2027MB], the GCFI-OS9 DISK[HFS], and the GCFI-OS9 DISK folders to display the list of directories located in the OS 9 root. Examine the folder structure, and note the differences between OS 9 and Windows.

6. Right-click the **Documents** folder, select **Export Files**, navigate to the C:\Work\ Labs\Evidence folder, and click **OK** to extract the files. Click **Close** in the Export Results dialog box (see Figure 8-5). Repeat this process for the **System** folder and the **Trash** folder. Disregard any error messages, and close the error dialog boxes if they appear. Click the **File** tab, and select **Exit** to close the FTK Imager application.

7. Right-click the **Forensic Toolkit 1.81** icon on your desktop, and click **Run as administrator**.

8

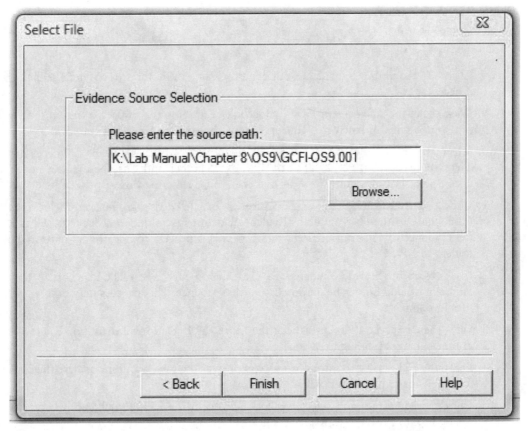

Figure 8-4   Select the OS 9 image file

Course Technology/Cengage Learning

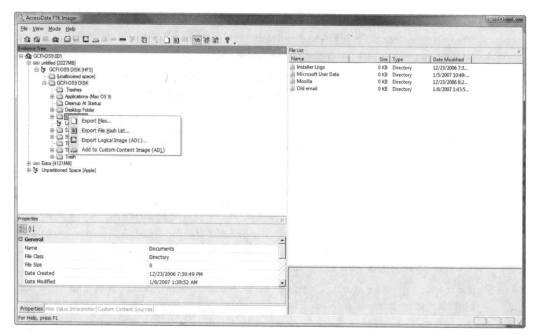

Figure 8-5   Export Documents files

Course Technology/Cengage Learning

8. Click **Allow** in the User Account dialog box. Click **OK** in the CodeMeter.exe dialog box, if necessary.

9. Click **OK** in the AccessData FTK dialog box describing the 5000 maximum limit in the trial version of this software. This error will appear each time you start FTK.

10. Select **Start a new case** in the AccessData FTK Startup dialog box, if necessary, and click **OK**. Type **C8Proj2** in both the Case Number and Case Name text boxes, and click **Next** six times until the Add Evidence to Case dialog box appears.

11. Click **Add Evidence**, select the **Contents of Folder** radio button, click **Continue** to navigate to the C:\Work\Labs\Evidence\Documents folder, and click **OK**. Click **OK** in the Evidence Information dialog box. Repeat this process to add the Systems and Trash folders to FTK.

12. Click **Next** in the Add Evidence to Case dialog box, and click **Finish** in the Case Summary dialog box to begin processing the evidence. This process may take a few minutes to complete.

13. Click the **Graphics** tab, and check the **List all descendants** box to view all the graphics images (see Figure 8-6).

14. Leave the FTK 1.81 program open as you answer the review questions. Use the FTK tabs to search for the information.

15. Click the **File** tab, and select **Exit**. Click **No** in the FTK Exit Backup Confirmation dialog box to close the FTK program.

Figure 8-6   Graphics files

Course Technology/Cengage Learning

Review Questions

1. How many files have bad extensions?

    a. 54

    b. 37

    c. 22

    d. 36

2. How many sent messages were located in this evidence?

    a. 22

    b. 54

    c. 76

    d. 37

3. How many e-mails involve Sebastian and Ileen? (*Hint:* Use the Cumulative Results in the Search tab.)

    a. 34

    b. 14

    c. 37

    d. 22

8

4. How many documents were recovered from the Trash folder?

   a. 22

   b. 1

   c. 0

   d. 37

5. How many files were recovered in this image?

   a. 3129

   b. 3368

   c. 3238

   d. 4

Lab 8.3 Using FTK Imager and the Forensic Toolkit to Process a Linux Image

Objectives

FTK Imager and FTK can be used to also process Linux ext3-formatted file systems. The ext3 file system is commonly used by many versions of the Linux kernel, and it is optimized to use less CPU process loading than previous versions. The journaling capability of this file system also provides excellent file recovery on corrupted or damaged disk drives. Because many companies seek alternative operating systems to lower the cost of licensing and because of the growth of open source applications such as Star Office, ext3 is gaining popularity. Forensics investigators may encounter images that are formatted in ext3, and although the FTK 1.81 is not designed to support this file system, FTK Imager can extract information that can be searched using Windows. In this lab, you will extract the Linux image and use FTK Imager to export files into FTK for analysis.

After completing this lab, you will be able to:

- Use FTK Imager to extract files located on an ext3 partition
- Analyze potential evidence located on a Linux partition

Materials Required

This lab requires the following:

- GCFI-LX.zip file
- FTK Imager
- Forensic Toolkit (FTK) 1.81
- Windows Vista

Estimated completion time: **15–20 minutes**

Activity

In this activity, you will extract the Linux image and import it into FTK Imager and FTK to process evidence.

1. Create a LINUX folder in the C:\Work\Labs\Chapter 8 folder. Navigate to the InChap8 folder on the student data disk, right-click the **GCFI-LX.zip** file, and click **Extract All**.

Click **Browse** in the Extract Compressed (Zipped) Folders dialog box, navigate to the C:\ Work\Labs\Chapter 8\LINUX folder, and click **Extract** to unzip the files to the folder.

2. Double-click the **FTK Imager** icon located on your desktop. When FTK Imager has finished loading, click the **File** tab, and select **Add Evidence Item**.

3. Select the **Image File** radio button in the Select Source dialog box, and click **Next**.

4. Click the **Browse** button, navigate to the C:\Work\Labs\Evidence\LINUX folder, select the **GCFI-LX.001** image, and click **Open**. Click **Finish** in the Select File dialog box.

5. In the upper-left Evidence Tree window, click the + symbols to expand the GCFI-LX.001, NONAME [Ext3], and [root] folders to display the list of directories located in the Linux partition (see Figure 8-7). Examine the folder structure, and note the differences between this image and the previous disk images.

6. Right-click the **home** folder, select **Export Files**, navigate to the C:\Work\Labs\ Evidence folder, and click **OK** in the Browse for Folder dialog box. Click **OK** in the Export Results dialog box. Repeat this process for the Var folder to export the files. Disregard any error messages, and close the Error dialog boxes if they appear. Click the **File** tab, and select **Exit** to close the FTK Imager application.

7. Right-click the **Forensic Toolkit 1.81** icon on your desktop, and click **Run as administrator**.

8. Click **Allow** in the User Account dialog box. Click **OK** in the CodeMeter.exe dialog box, if necessary.

9. Click **OK** in the AccessData FTK dialog box describing the 5000 maximum limit in the trial version of this software. This error will appear each time you start FTK.

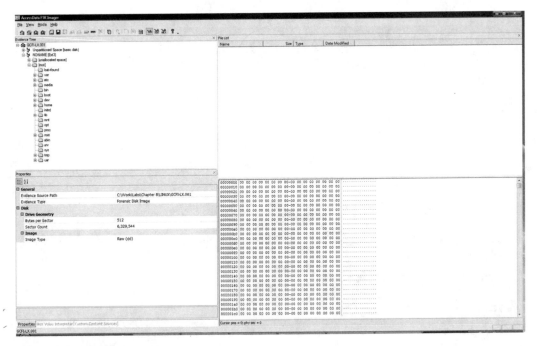

Figure 8-7   Linux partition

Course Technology/Cengage Learning

10. Select **Start a new case** in the AccessData FTK Startup dialog box, if necessary, and click **OK**. Type **C8Proj3** in both the Case Number and Case Name text boxes, and click **Next** six times until the Add Evidence to Case dialog box appears.

11. Click **Add Evidence**, select the **Contents of Folder** radio button, click **Continue**, and navigate to the C:\Work\Labs\Evidence folder. Click the **home** folder, and click **OK** in the Browse for Folder dialog box. Click **OK** in the Evidence Information dialog box. Repeat this process to export the files from the Var folder.

12. Click **Next** in the Add Evidence to Case dialog box, and click **Finish** in the Case Summary dialog box to begin processing the evidence. This process may take a few minutes to complete. Disregard the warning that this evidence exceeded the 5000 object limit.

13. Verify that the evidence list in the lower window contains the Home and Var folders. Normally the entire disk image could be processed by FTK; however, the trial version of this software included with this lab manual is limited to 5000 items and the remaining objects will be discarded. This will not affect the results of your lab.

14. Click the **Graphics** tab, and check the **List all descendants** box to view all the graphics images (see Figure 8-8).

15. Click the **E-Mail** tab to view the e-mail accounts on this image, and click each folder to view e-mail messages.

16. Leave the FTK 1.81 program open as you answer the review questions for this lab. Use the FTK tabs to search for the information.

17. Click the **File** tab, and select **Exit**. Click **No** in the FTK Exit Backup Confirmation dialog box to close the FTK program.

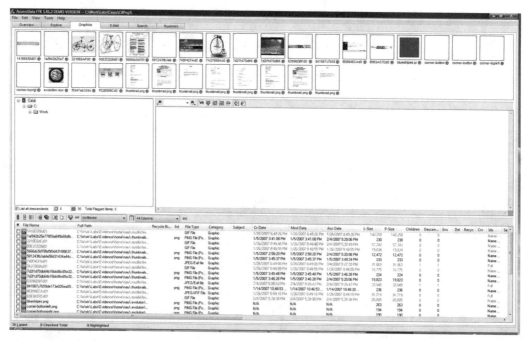

Figure 8-8   Linux graphics images

Course Technology/Cengage Learning

Review Questions

1. How many e-mail messages did Nau Tjeriko send?

    a. 27

    b. 154

    c. 59

    d. 31

    email sent

2. How many Windows Media .wmv files were recovered in this image?

    a. 8

    b. 4

    c. 30

    d. 3

    over multimedia

3. How many graphics files have bad extensions but are still viewable?

    a. 31

    b. 30

    c. 9

    d. 3

    overview click

    All

4. How many graphics images are .gif files?

    a. 5

    b. 30

    c. 9

    d. 3

    graphics tab

5. Why is the Total File Items count displaying 5000?

    a. This number represents the total number of files in the Linux image.

    b. This number represents the maximum number of objects that the trial version of FTK can process.

    c. This number represents the total number of objects in the Home and Var folders.

    d. This number represents the number of files recovered from the Recycle Bin.

COMPUTER FORENSICS ANALYSIS AND VALIDATION

Labs included in this chapter

- Lab 9.1 Searching for Hidden Partitions
- Lab 9.2 Looking for Evidence in Hidden Partitions
- Lab 9.3 Examining the Original Evidence with Forensic Toolkit

Lab 9.1 Searching for Hidden Partitions

Objectives

The search for computer crimes often involves recovering data from hidden or deliberately modified disk partitions where the criminal might store potential evidence. In some cases, criminals hide data by formatting different file systems on a single physical disk. For example, a hard disk might have two partitions where the first partition is formatted in NTFS and the second partition is formatted in HFS or some other file system unreadable by Windows. In this situation, an examiner looking for evidence using Windows Explorer will only see the first NTFS partition and its associated files but will not see the second partition unless the storage device is viewed using the Disk Management feature. The Disk Management utility will only identify the second partition as "Healthy" without providing any file system details. You have seen in previous labs that FTK Imager can view Windows, Macintosh, and Linux file partitions and perform preliminary searches for files. In this lab, you will examine evidence gathered from a USB flash drive attached to a Windows computer to locate hidden partitions not visible in Windows.

After completing this lab, you will be able to:

- Look for hidden partitions on storage devices
- Use FTK Imager to extract non-Windows-based file evidence

Materials Required

This lab requires the following:

- Windows Vista
- C9Proj01.E01
- FTK Imager

Estimated completion time: **15–20 minutes**

Activity

In this activity, you will add the C9Proj1.E01 image file to FTK Imager to look for multiple disk partitions.

1. Create a **Chapter 9** folder in your C:/Work/Labs folder, and copy the C9Proj1.E01, C9Proj1.E01.csv, and C9Proj1.E01.txt files from the InChap9 folder on your student data disk to the C:/Work/Labs/Chapter 9 folder.

2. Double-click the **FTK Imager** icon located on your desktop.

3. Click the **File** tab, and click **Add Evidence Item**.

4. Click **Image File** in the Select Source dialog box, and click **Next**.

5. In the Select File dialog box, click **Browse** and navigate to the C:\Work\Labs\Chapter 9 folder. Click the **C9Proj1.E01** image file, and click **Open**. Do not select the .csv or .txt files with the same name; they will be used later.

6. Click **Finish** in the Select File dialog box.

7. Click all the + symbols to expand the folders in the C9Proj1.E01 icon in the upper-left evidence tree window, and note the three disk partitions listed (see Figure 9-1).

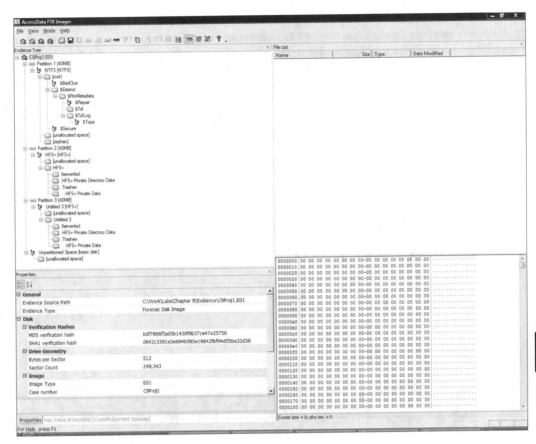

Figure 9-1 C9Proj1.E01 partitions

Course Technology/Cengage Learning

8. Click the **[root]** folder located in the Partition 1 section, and note the evidence files in the upper-right File List window. Select the **Eyeglass** icon on the tool bar if necessary, and click each file to view them using the built-in file viewer in the lower right window.

9. Create an **Evidence** folder in the C:\Work\Labs\Chapter 9 folder. Right-click the **[root]** folder, select **Export Files**, navigate to the C:\Work\Labs\Chapter 9\Evidence folder, and click **OK** in the Browse for Folder dialog box to send the exported files to the Evidence folder. Close the Exported Results dialog box by clicking **OK**. The exported files will be located in the [root] folder within the Evidence folder. Right-click the Windows **Start** button, and select **Explore** to launch Windows Explorer. Click the **Tools** tab, select **Folder Options**, and click the **View** tab in the Folder Options dialog box. Click **Show hidden files and folders**, uncheck the **Hide extensions for known file types** check box, and uncheck the **Hide protected operating system files (Recommended)** check box. Click **Yes** in the Warning dialog box, click **Apply**, and click **OK** in the Folder Options dialog box. You can now browse the [root] folder using Windows Explorer.

10. Click the **HFS+** folder located under the Partition 2 drive icon in the second non–Windows partition. Browse each file to view it using the Eyeglass file viewer. When you are finished, right-click the **HFS+** folder, select **Export Files**, navigate to C:\Work\Labs\Chapter 9\ Evidence folder, and click **OK** in the Browse for Folder dialog box to export the files and folders using the same procedure as Step 9. Click **Close** in the Export Results dialog box and disregard any error messages.

11. Right-click the **Untitled 3 [HFS+]** folder located in the third partition (labeled Partition 3), select **Export Files**, navigate to the C:\Work\Labs\Chapter 9\Evidence folder, and click **OK** in the Browse for Folder dialog box. Click **Close** in the Export Results dialog box and disregard any error messages.

12. Navigate to the C:\Work\Labs\Chapter 9\Evidence folder using Windows Explorer, and verify that it contains the [root], HFS+, and Untitled 3 folders containing the exported evidence files along with the C9Proj1.E01, C9Proj1.E01.csv, and C9Proj1.E01.txt files (see Figure 9-2). The exported files will be examined and compared in Labs 9.2 and 9.3. You may close Windows Explorer.

13. Click the **C9Proj1.E01** image located at the top of the Evidence Tree in the upper-left window, and locate the Verification Hashes section in the lower-left Properties window to view the MD5 and SHA1 verification hashes. Minimize the AccessData FTK Imager program by clicking the **Restore Down** icon.

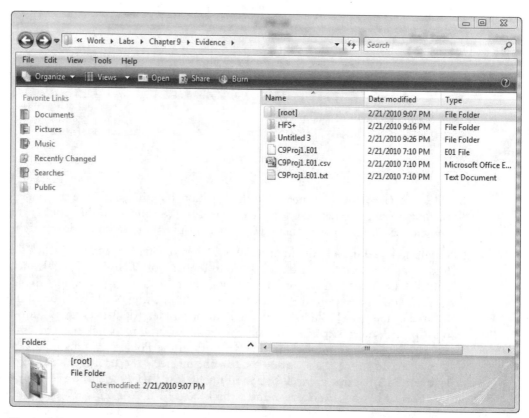

Figure 9-2   Evidence folder contents

Course Technology/Cengage Learning

Figure 9-3 C9Proj1.E01.txt

Course Technology/Cengage Learning

14. Double-click the **C9Proj1.E01.txt** file in the C:\Work\Labs\Chapter 9\Evidence folder, and double-click the **C9Proj1.E01.txt** file to open it in Notepad (see Figure 9-3). Minimize the window by clicking the **Restore Down** icon. Place the text document next to the window created in Step 13 to compare the computed hashes in the text document with the Verification Hashes in FTK Imager. They should match, indicating that the processed image is forensically identical to the recovered image from the seized storage device.

15. Leave the FTK Imager and the text file open while you answer the review questions for this lab.

16. Click the **File** tab in FTK Imager, and select **Exit** to close FTK Imager. Close the C9Proj1.E01.txt file.

Review Questions

1. How many sectors were discovered on the forensic image?

    a. 63

    b. 512

    • c. 249,343

    d. 255

2. How many formatted partitions were recovered in the forensic image?

    a. 2

    b. 4

    c. 1

    • d. 3

3. What is the starting sector for Partition 2?

    • a. 83,286

    b. 83,032

    c. 63

    d. 166,320

4. Assuming contiguous sector blocks, how many sectors exist between Partition 1 and Partition 2?

    a. 63

    b. 254

    c. 82,971

    • d. 15

5. What are the cluster sizes for each of the partitions?

    • a. 4,096

    b. 10,400

    c. 8,407

    d. 10,379

Lab 9.2 Looking for Evidence in Hidden Partitions

Objectives

In the previous lab, you searched for hidden partitions on a USB device attached to a Windows computer. Because Windows does not read or write to non-Windows-formatted partitions, the existence of any partition other than FAT, FAT32, and NTFS on a single storage device suggests that potential evidence may be hidden. In this lab, you will start a new Forensic Toolkit (FTK) case and add the exported files from all three partitions located on the USB device.

After completing this lab, you will be able to:

- Add the exported files to FTK for analysis
- Compare the hash values of exported evidence to look for duplicate files

Materials Required

This lab requires the following:

- The three exported folders from Lab 9.1
- Forensic Toolkit (FTK) 1.81
- Windows Vista

Estimated completion time: **15–20 minutes**

Activity

In this lab, you will add the three exported folders to FTK.

1. Log on to Windows Vista as the administrator. Right-click the **Forensic Toolkit 1.81** icon on your desktop, and click **Run as administrator**.

2. Click **Allow** in the User Account Control dialog box. Click **OK** in the CodeMeter.exe dialog box, if necessary.

3. Click **OK** in the AccessData FTK dialog box describing the 5000 maximum limit in the trial version of this software. This error will appear each time you start FTK.

4. Select **Start a new case** in the AccessData FTK Startup dialog box, if necessary, and click **OK**. Type **C9Proj2** in the Case Number and Case Name boxes. Click **Next** six times.

5. Click **Add Evidence** in the Add Evidence to Case dialog box, select **Contents of a Folder**, and click **Continue** to browse to the C:\Work\Labs\Chapter 9\Evidence folder. Select the **[root]** folder, and click **OK**.

6. Type **NTFS** in the Evidence Identification Name/Number text box located in the Evidence Information dialog box, and click **OK**.

7. Click **Add Evidence** in the Add Evidence to Case dialog box, select **Contents of a Folder**, and click **Continue** to browse to the C:\Work\Labs\Chapter 9\Evidence folder. Select the **HFS+** folder, and click **OK**.

8. Type **HFS+** in the Evidence Identification Name/Number text box located in the Evidence Information dialog box, and click **OK**.

9. Click **Add Evidence** in the Add Evidence to Case dialog box, select **Contents of a Folder**, and click **Continue** to browse to the C:\Work\Labs\Chapter 9\Evidence folder. Select the **Untitled 3** folder, and click **OK**.

10. Type **Untitled 3** in the Evidence Identification Name/Number text box located in the Evidence Information dialog box, and click **OK**.

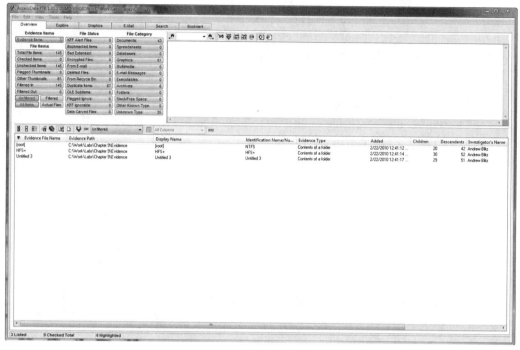

Figure 9-4 FTK with the added evidence

Course Technology/Cengage Learning

11. Click **Next** in the Add Evidence to Case dialog box to continue, and click **Finish** in the Case Summary dialog box. FTK will process and index the exported files, and it may take a few minutes to finish. Your screen should look like Figure 9-4. In the lower window the three folders that were exported from the USB flash drive will be listed, and all the evidence files recovered from the USB flash drive will be located in their respective file type buckets under the File Category column.

12. Click the **Explore** tab, and expand the **Work, Labs, Chapter 9**, and **Evidence** folders to locate the [root], HFS+, and Untitled 3 exported folders that were recovered from the USB evidence.

13. Click the **[root]** folder, and notice the evidence files located in the lower window.

14. Click the **f6.jpg** file, and view the image in the upper-right window (see Figure 9-5). These files were located on the NTFS partition that was visible when viewed using Windows Explorer.

15. Click the **HFS+** folder, and notice all the evidence located on the OS X HFS+ partition. Drag the bottom scroll bar to the right to view the file attributes along with their respective MD5 and SHA1 hashes (see Figure 9-6). These files would not be visible in Windows Explorer.

16. Click the **Untitled 3** folder, and notice that the files listed with the exception of the first journal are grayed out (i.e., the attribute descriptions are in a light font color), indicating that these files were located on an unrecognizable or hidden partition. Click any image file, and notice that it can still be seen in the image viewer.

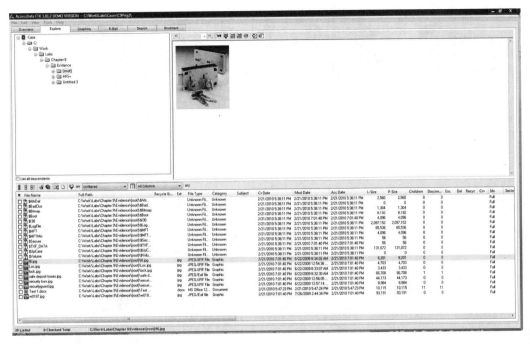

Figure 9-5 Evidence on NTFS partition

Course Technology/Cengage Learning

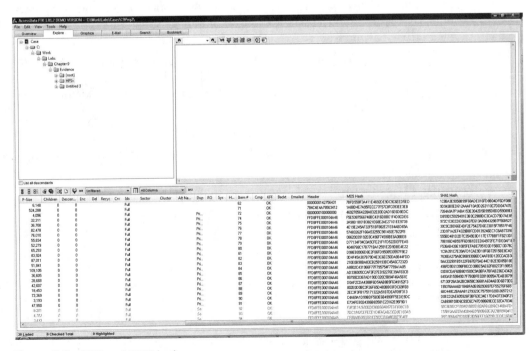

Figure 9-6 MD5 and SHA1 hashes

Course Technology/Cengage Learning

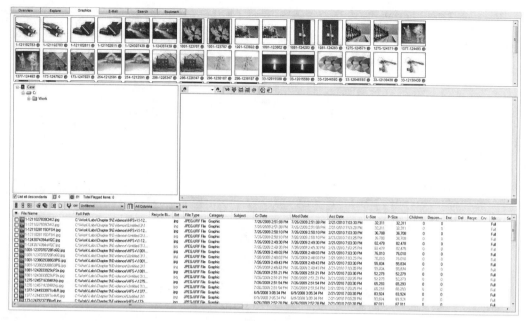

Figure 9-7 Graphics images

Course Technology/Cengage Learning

17. Click the **Graphics** tab, and click the **List all descendants** check box. The images located in all the partitions will be displayed (see Figure 9-7). Drag the upper-right scroll bar to view all the images. Notice that some images have two copies, whereas others have three duplicate copies. The latter indicates that duplicate images were located on all three partitions.

18. In the middle left window, expand the **Work, Labs, Chapter 9**, and **Evidence** folders in the evidence tree. Click the **[root]** folder to display the images located on the first NTFS partition. Now click the **HFS+** and **Untitled 3** folders, and notice the duplicated files existing on both partitions.

19. Leave FTK open while you answer the review questions for this lab.

20. Close FTK, and in the FTK Exit Backup Confirmation dialog box, click **No**.

Review Questions

1. How many images were recovered in the NTFS partition?
   - a. 7
   - b. 61
   - c. 27
   - d. 13

2. How many images in total were recovered from the USB evidence?

    a. 27

    b. 13

    c. 61

    d. 7

3. How many duplicate items were located on this evidence?

    a. 61

    b. 13

    c. 7

    d. 87

4. How many document files were located on this evidence?

    a. 61

    b. 145

    c. 43

    d. 61

5. How many copies of the f6.jpg file were located on this evidence?

    a. 2

    b. 3

    c. 1

    d. 7

Lab 9.3 Examining the Original Evidence with Forensic Toolkit

Objectives

The USB evidence presented in this chapter contained two hidden partitions with potential evidence that might have been overlooked. Forensics investigators should become familiar with multiple discovery tools because one tool may not find all the evidence or support multiple file systems in use on storage devices. You have learned that criminals often save potential evidence in corrupt or hidden partitions to hide them from investigators assuming that only one file system is in use within a hard drive or other storage media. In this lab, you will examine the original forensic image recovered at a crime scene and compare the results with the previous lab exercise results to determine how much information might have been missed if the investigator only used one forensic tool.

After completing this lab, you will be able to:

- Process evidence with multiple partitions
- Recognize non-Windows partitions

Materials Required

This lab requires the following:

- Windows Vista
- Forensic Toolkit (FTK) 1.81
- C9Proj1.E01 image

Estimated completion time: **20–30 minutes**

Activity

In this activity, you will add the original USB image directly to FTK.

1. Right-click the **Forensic Toolkit 1.81** icon on your desktop, and click **Run as administrator**.

2. Click **Allow** in the User Account dialog box. Click **OK** in the CodeMeter.exe dialog box, if necessary.

3. Click **OK** in the AccessData FTK dialog box describing the 5000 maximum limit in the trial version of this software. This error will appear each time you start FTK.

4. Select **Start a new case** in the AccessData FTK Startup dialog box, if necessary, and click **OK**. Type **C9Proj3** in the Case Number and Case Name boxes, and click **Next** six times.

5. Click **Add Evidence** in the Add Evidence to Case dialog box, select **Acquired Image of Drive**, and click **Continue** to browse to the C:\Work\Labs\Chapter 9\Evidence folder. Select the **C9Proj1.E01** image file, and click **Open**.

6. In the Evidence Information dialog box, type **C9Proj3** in the Evidence Identification Name/Number text box, and click **OK**. Verify the three partitions and the unpartitioned space all have been added as evidence (see Figure 9-8). Click **Next** and **Finish** in the Case Summary dialog box. The evidence should be processed in a minute or two.

7. Click the **Explore** tab, and notice that Part 1 is listed as an NTFS partition and both Part 2 and Part 3 partitions are listed as NONAME-Unknown.

8. Click the **NTFS-NTFS** folder, and locate all the image files recovered in this partition (see Figure 9-9). Drag the lower window up if necessary to view all the files.

9. Click the **Graphics** tab, and select the **List all descendants** check box. Note the only recovered images depicted in the top window located on the USB evidence.

10. Click the **Overview** tab, and examine the file contents in each of the buckets located under the File Category column.

11. Leave FTK open as you answer the review questions for this lab.

12. Close FTK, and in the FTK Exit Backup Confirmation dialog box, click **No**.

Figure 9-8   Added evidence

Course Technology/Cengage Learning

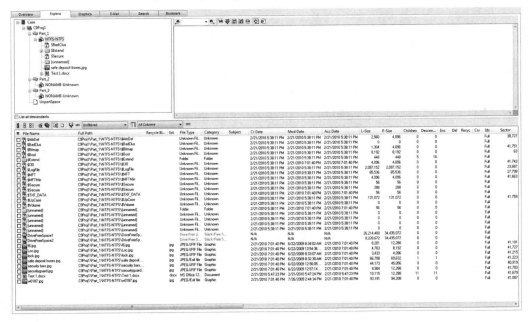

Figure 9-9   NTFS files

Course Technology/Cengage Learning

Review Questions

1. How many total graphics images were located on this evidence?

   a. 13

   b. 66

   • c. 7

   d. 33

2. How many MS Word documents were recovered on this evidence?

   a. 13

   b. 66

   c. 7

   • d. 1

3. What is the physical size of the Part 2 partition (verify the List all descendants check box is checked)?

   a. 42,512,384

   b. 42,481,152

   c. 26,214,400

   • d. 16,297,984

4. What is the physical size of the MBR? (*Hint:* Look in the UnpartSpace.)

   a. 67,072

   • b. 512

   c. 26,214,400

   d. 42,481,152

5. Why did FTK not find the additional files recovered in the previous lab?

   a. FTK did not process this evidence correctly.

   b. Unpartitioned space cannot be searched by FTK.

   • c. FTK does not support Linux- and Macintosh-formatted partitions.

   d. FTK can only read the first formatted partition.

RECOVERING GRAPHICS FILES

Labs included in this chapter

- Lab 10.1 Viewing Evidence at the Crime Scene
- Lab 10.2 Processing Evidence Containing Graphics Images
- Lab 10.3 Locating Graphics in Unreadable Partitions

Lab 10.1 Viewing Evidence at the Crime Scene

Objectives

You have been summoned to a crime scene to help recover potential evidence found on a booted computer. On initial examination you see several files that have suspicious file extensions, and they are not able to be viewed in Windows Explorer. Experience tells you that there may be potential evidence hidden from view, and your job is to find any usable data. In this lab, you will examine the evidence using Windows Explorer to see why the investigator became suspicious and decided to process this evidence.

After completing this lab, you will be able to:

- Look for suspicious files
- Identify incorrect or inconsistent file types

Materials Required

This lab requires the following:

- Windows Vista
- MS Office 2007
- NTFS folder

Estimated completion time: **10–15 minutes**

Activity

In this activity, you will examine the NTFS folder and record the observed files.

1. Create a **Chapter 10** folder in your C:\Work\Labs location.

2. Copy the **NTFS** folder located in the InChap10 folder on the student data disk to your C:\Work\Labs\Chapter 10 folder.

3. Double-click the **NTFS** folder to see the files located in the USB flash drive.

4. Double-click the **Fig07-04.jpg** file in the NTFS folder to view the image in Windows Photo Gallery (see Figure 10-1).

5. Use the **Next** button in the Windows Photo Gallery to view all the other image files located on this USB flash drive, and write down the file name displayed in the upper-left corner. Answer Review Question 1 using the information you just recorded.

6. After you reach the last image (see Figure 10-2), the viewer will return back to the first file you viewed. Close the Windows Photo Gallery application.

7. Double-click the **temp.doc** file in the NTFS folder, and notice that it does not open MS Word as expected, although the file icon indicates it is an MS Word document. Click **Cancel** in the File Conversion-temp.doc dialog window.

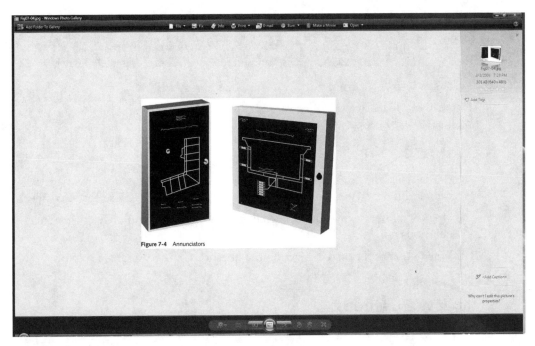

Figure 10-1 Image file

Course Technology/Cengage Learning

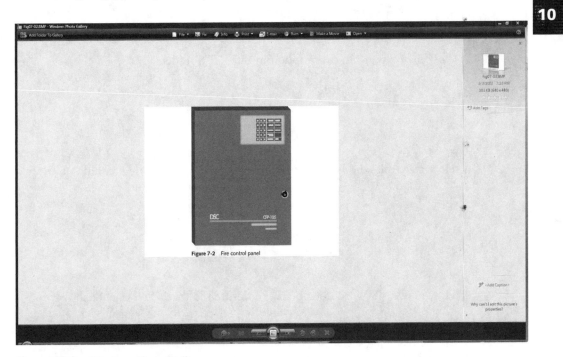

Figure 10-2 Windows Photo Gallery

Course Technology/Cengage Learning

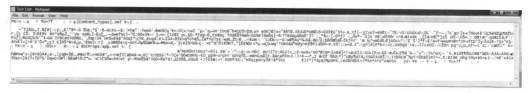

Figure 10-3   Test 1.txt

Course Technology/Cengage Learning

8. Double-click the **Test 1.txt** file in the NTFS folder, and note that Notepad displays a file with ASCII characters that is unreadable (see Figure 10-3). Close Test 1.txt file in Notepad.

9. Open Windows Explorer, double-click each file listed, and answer the remaining review questions.

10. When you are finished answering the questions, close Windows Explorer.

Review Questions

1. How many viewable images were located in the NTFS folder?

   a. 6

   b. 3

   c. 5

   d. 11

2. How many total files were found in the NTFS folder?

   a. 9

   b. 7

   c. 10

   d. 11

3. How many files did Windows Explorer fail to open because it could not locate the associated program?

   a. 2

   b. 3

   c. 5

   d. 11

4. How many MS Word documents are located in the NTFS USB flash drive?

   a. 3

   b. 5

   c. 11

   d. 2

5. How many valid graphics file types did you locate on this USB flash drive?

a. 3

b. 2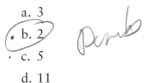

c. 5

d. 11

Lab 10.2 Processing Evidence Containing Graphics Images

Objectives

After your initial inspection of the USB evidence at the crime scene, an image of the drive must be created and processed by Forensic Toolkit (FTK) to recover any additional evidence. The files viewed in Windows Explorer in Lab 10.1 might not be the only potential evidence located on this drive; as such, the drive will now be searched again using FTK. The InChap10.001 image file will be added to FTK and processed in this lab.

After completing this lab, you will be able to:

- Examine files that have bad extensions
- Identify JPEG header signatures

Materials Required

This lab requires the following:

- Windows Vista
- InChap10.001 image file
- Forensic Toolkit (FTK) 1.81

Estimated completion time: **15–20 minutes**

Activity

In this lab, you will add the InChap10.001 image file as evidence to FTK and locate the graphics files contained in the evidence.

1. Copy the InChap10.001 image file located in the InChap10 folder on the student data disk to your C:\Work\Labs\Chapter 10 folder.

2. Right-click the **Forensic Toolkit 1.81** icon on your desktop, and click **Run as administrator**. Click **Allow** in the User Account Control dialog box, and click **OK** in the CodeMeter.exe dialog box, if necessary.

3. Click **OK** in the AccessData FTK dialog box warning you that only a maximum of 5000 objects can be analyzed.

4. Select **Start a new case** in the AccessData FTK Startup dialog box, if necessary, and click **OK**.

5. Type **C10Proj2** in both the Case Number and Case Name boxes in the New Case dialog box, and click **Next** six times until the Add Evidence to Case dialog box appears.

Figure 10-4   InChap10.001 image file

Course Technology/Cengage Learning

6. Click **Add Evidence**, and click **Acquired Image of Drive**, if necessary, in the Add Evidence to Case dialog box. Click **Continue**, and navigate to the C:\Work\ Labs\Chapter 10 folder. Click on the InChap10.001 image file, and click **Open** (see Figure 10-4).

7. Click **OK** in the Evidence Information dialog box, and click **Next** in the Add Evidence to Case dialog box. Click **Finish** in the Case Summary dialog box.

8. With the Overview tab selected, click the **Bad Extension** bucket to see all the files that have deliberately changed file extensions inconsistent with their associated file types.

9. Click the **Deleted Files** bucket, and locate the files deleted from the USB evidence. Verify that the **Eyeglass** icon is selected in the tool bar, and click each deleted file to view it. Note the red X icon next to each file indicating that they were deleted.

10. Click the **Graphics** tab, and check the **List all descendants** check box to view all the recovered graphics images located on the USB evidence (see Figure 10-5). The files listed with the red font color in the bottom window have bad file extensions.

11. Right-click the **03x07.bmt** file, and click **File Properties** to view the current file extension and its true file type. Close the File Properties dialog box.

12. Click the **temp.doc** file, and notice that the MS Word document is a JPEG image file instead of a document.

13. Click the bottom scroll bar, and drag it to the right to see the selected file header. The FFD8FFE header also verifies the file is a JPEG image file and not a document file (see Figure 10-6). Also note the Y under the Badxt column, indicating that the file has a bad extension.

14. Leave FTK open as you answer the review questions for this lab.

15. Close FTK, and click **No** when prompted to back up the case file.

Figure 10-5   Recovered graphics

Course Technology/Cengage Learning

Figure 10-6   Temp.doc file

Course Technology/Cengage Learning

Review Questions

1. How many graphics files were located in the forensic image?

   a. 20

   b. 17

   c. 11

   d. 5

2. How many bad extension files were images?

   a. 8

   b. 5

   c. 7

   d. 11

3. How many deleted files were image files?

   a. 8

   b. 11

   c. 17

   d. 7

4. When was the temp.doc modified?

   a. 4/9/2009 at 4:03 PM

   b. 4/18/2010 at 8:09 PM

   c. 2/21/2010 at 7:01 PM

   d. 6/22/2009 at 8:34 AM

5. What type of file is the Text 1.txt file?

   a. Image file

   b. Text file

   c. MS Office 2007 file

   d. Hypertext .htm file

Lab 10.3 Locating Graphics in Unreadable Partitions

Objectives

Forensic evidence is often hidden by criminals using various methods on deliberately corrupted or modified partitions to make it invisible to all but the creator of the file. One of the most common methods used to hide data is to modify the file properties such as the header or file extension. For example, the file header that identifies the file type to the file system can be altered using a hex editor rendering it unreadable by the operating system. In some cases, the file can be overlooked by forensic software unless the investigator knows how to apply special features such as data carving to rebuild corrupt file attributes. In this lab, you will apply the data-carving feature to rebuild files that have been deliberately altered.

After completing this lab, you will be able to:

- Add data carving to repair damaged file attributes
- Recover data lost in hidden files

Materials Required

This lab requires the following:

- Windows Vista
- Forensic Toolkit (FTK) 1.81
- C10unreadable.001 image file

> Estimated completion time: **30–40 minutes**

Activity

In this activity, you will use a protocol analyzer to capture FTP traffic and analyze the results.

1. Copy the C10unreadable.001 image file located in the InChap10 folder on the student data disk to your C:\Work\Labs\Chapter 10 folder.

2. Right-click the **Forensic Toolkit 1.81** icon on your desktop, and click **Run as administrator**. Click **Allow** in the User Account Control dialog box, and click **OK** in the CodeMeter.exe dialog box, if necessary.

3. Click **OK** in the AccessData FTK dialog box warning you that only a maximum of 5000 objects can be analyzed.

4. Select **Start a new case**, if necessary, in the AccessData FTK Startup dialog box, and click **OK**.

5. Type **C10Proj3** in both the Case Number and Case Name boxes in the New Case dialog box, and click **Next** three times until the Evidence Processing Options dialog box appears.

6. Check the **Data Carve** box in the Evidence Processing Options dialog box, and click the **Carving Options** button to see all the supported graphics file types that may be recovered by carving data existing in unallocated disk space. Click **OK** to close the Data Carving dialog box, and click **Next** three times until the Add Evidence to Case dialog box appears.

7. Click the **Add Evidence** button in the Add Evidence to Case dialog box, select **Acquired Image of Drive**, if necessary, in the Add Evidence to Case dialog box, and click **Continue**. Navigate to the C10unreadable.001 image file located in the C:\Work\Labs\Chapter 10\folder, click on it, and click **Open**. In the Evidence Information dialog box, select **Eastern Time with Daylight Saving** in the Local Evidence Time Zone drop-down list (see Figure 10-7), and click **OK**.

8. Click **Next** in the Add Evidence to Case dialog box. Click **Finish** in the Case Summary dialog box.

Figure 10-7 Local Evidence Time Zone

Course Technology/Cengage Learning

9. Click the **Deleted Files** bucket to see all the deleted files that were located on the previously unreadable USB flash drive.

10. Notice the first two deleted files contain corrupt file paths (as depicted with symbols in the path names) and only one image file was recovered by carving the data from unallocated space (see Figure 10-8).

11. Click the **Bad Extension** bucket to see the modified file extension and its correctly recovered file header. Click the file to see the image in the viewer.

12. Click the **Graphics** tab, and check the **List all descendants** check box to see all the recovered images. One image was not completely repaired; however, the file attributes were recovered (see Figure 10-9).

13. Leave FTK open as you answer the review questions for this lab.

14. Close FTK, and click **No** when prompted to back up the case file.

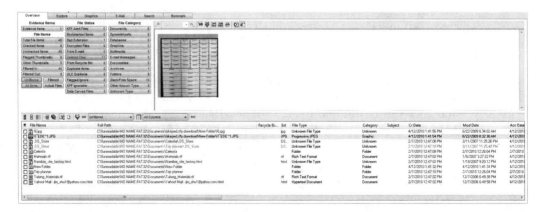

Figure 10-8 Carved files

Course Technology/Cengage Learning

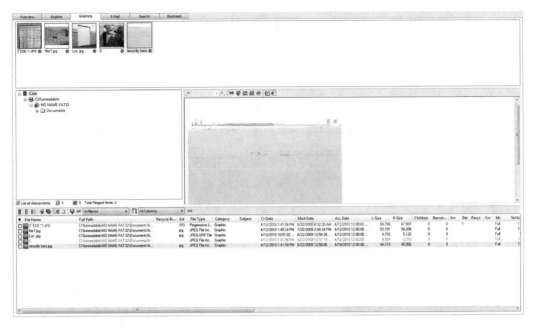

Figure 10-9 Recovered graphics

Course Technology/Cengage Learning

Review Questions

1. What is the file system in use on the recovered evidence?

   a. MS-DOS

   b. NTFS

   c. FAT32

   d. HFS+

2. In what sector was the bad extension image file located?

   a. 17,428

   b. 8,984

   c. 9,216

   d. 4,620

3. How many deleted files were recovered by the data-carving process?

   a. 8

   b. 5

   c. 11

   d. 40

(11) - John West

4. How many deleted folders were discovered in this evidence?

   a. 3

   b. 8

   c. 40

   d. 10

5. How many deleted document files were recovered from the carved data?

   a. 8

   b. 3

   c. 11

   d. 5

11- 3 folders : 8

John-westly

VIRTUAL MACHINES, NETWORK FORENSICS, AND LIVE ACQUISITIONS

Labs included in this chapter

- Lab 11.1 Using a Live Acquisition Tool to Capture Evidence
- Lab 11.2 Analyzing Virtual Memory Using Forensic Toolkit
- Lab 11.3 Analyzing Windows Registry

Lab 11.1 Using a Live Acquisition Tool to Capture Evidence

Objectives

You have used AccessData's Forensic Toolkit (FTK) Imager to image storage devices, provide preliminary forensic information, and analyze several file system partitions. However, FTK Imager is also available in a portable version that will fit on a small USB storage device, and it can be used to acquire the contents of virtual memory and the Windows registry. The virtual memory and Windows registry contain useful information that may be related to any computer crimes committed on that machine. For example, the virtual memory holds data temporarily as the operating system processes instructions. Often information about recently attached devices such as physical storage devices, external storage devices, or computer hardware may be found in the registry.

After completing this lab, you will be able to:

- Create a portable forensic recovery tool
- Perform a live acquisition of the Windows registry

Materials Required

This lab requires the following:

- Windows Vista
- FTK Imager Lite 2.9.0 zip
- An unused 128-MB or larger USB flash drive

Estimated completion time: **15–20 minutes**

Activity

In this activity, you will install FTK Imager Lite onto a USB flash drive and use it to capture the Windows registry files.

1. Create a **Chapter 11** folder in your C:\Work\Labs folder.

2. Locate the **Imager Lite 2.9.0.zip** file in the InChap11 folder on the student data disk, and copy the file to the Chapter 11 folder you created in the C:\Work\Labs folder.

3. Insert the USB flash drive into your computer, and allow Windows Vista to identify the device and load the drivers. After Windows has finished installing the flash drive, click the **Start** button, and click **Computer** to open Windows Explorer.

4. Right-click the USB flash drive, and select **Format** from the context menu. Select **FAT32** in the File system box, and type **FTKImager** in the Volume label box (see Figure 11-1). In the Format dialog box, click **Start** to format the drive, and prepare it for FTK Imager Lite. Click **OK** in the Format warning dialog box to continue.

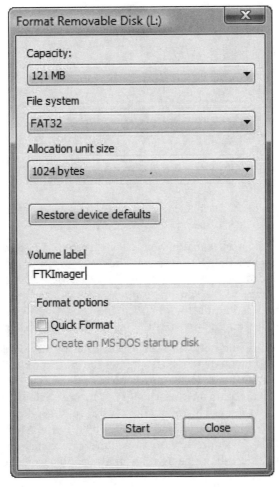

Figure 11-1   Format USB flash drive
Course Technology/Cengage Learning

5. After the format is complete, click **OK** in the Format Complete dialog box. In the Format FTK IMAGER dialog box, note the assigned drive letter in the title bar. Click **Close** to exit the format utility.

6. Navigate to the **C:\Work\Labs\Chapter 11** folder, and locate the **Imager Lite 2.9.0.zip** file. Right-click the file, and select **Extract All**.

7. In the Extract Compressed (Zipped) Folders, click **Browse**, locate the FTKImager USB flash drive you formatted, and click **Extract** to uncompress the zipped files into the FTKImager USB flash drive.

8. After the files have been added to the USB flash drive, the file list will display (see Figure 11-2). Double-click the **FTK Imager.exe** file to start the software.

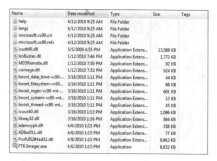

Name	Date modified	Type	Size	Tags
help	4/12/2010 9:25 AM	File Folder		
langs	4/12/2010 9:25 AM	File Folder		
microsoft.vc90.crt	4/12/2010 9:25 AM	File Folder		
microsoft.vc90.mfc	4/12/2010 9:25 AM	File Folder		
icudt40.dll	5/5/2009 4:55 PM	Application Extens...	13,588 KB	
IsoBuster.dll	1/12/2010 7:46 PM	Application Extens...	1,773 KB	
MD5Remote.dll	1/12/2010 7:50 PM	Application Extens...	92 KB	
cximage.dll	1/12/2010 7:52 PM	Application Extens...	924 KB	
boost_date_time-vc90-...	3/16/2010 1:11 PM	Application Extens...	44 KB	
boost_filesystem-vc90...	3/16/2010 1:11 PM	Application Extens...	66 KB	
boost_regex-vc90-mt-...	3/16/2010 1:11 PM	Application Extens...	601 KB	
boost_system-vc90-mt...	3/16/2010 1:11 PM	Application Extens...	13 KB	
boost_thread-vc90-mt...	3/16/2010 1:11 PM	Application Extens...	45 KB	
icuuc40.dll	3/16/2010 1:13 PM	Application Extens...	1,096 KB	
libeay32.dll	3/16/2010 1:16 PM	Application Extens...	994 KB	
adencrypt.dll	4/6/2010 1:15 PM	Application Extens...	338 KB	
ADIsoDLL.dll	4/6/2010 1:15 PM	Application Extens...	77 KB	
ProfUIS284ad32.dll	4/6/2010 1:15 PM	Application Extens...	9,862 KB	
FTK Imager.exe	4/6/2010 1:15 PM	Application	8,832 KB	

Figure 11-2 USB file list

Course Technology/Cengage Learning

9. Click **Continue** in the User Account Control dialog box. After FTK Imager loads, click the **File** tab, and click **Obtain Protected Files**.

10. In the Obtain System Files dialog box, click **Password recovery and all registry files** under the Options area. Click **Browse**, and select the **C:\Work\Labs\ Chapter 11** location in the Browse for Folder dialog box. Click **Make New Folder**, and type **Registry** in the edit name box. Click **OK**, and the path you created will be displayed in the Destination for obtained files box (see Figure 11-3). Click **OK** in the Obtain System Files dialog box, and the registry files will be copied.

11. Click the **File** tab, and click **Capture Memory**. In the Memory Capture dialog box, click **Browse**, and navigate to the **C:\Work\Labs\Chapter 11** folder. In the Browse for Folder dialog box, click **Make New Folder**, and type **RAM** in the Folder text box. Click **OK** to add the path in the Memory Capture dialog box (see Figure 11-4).and click **Capture Memory**. This may take several minutes depending on the size of your installed RAM. When the Status indicates [100%] in the Memory Progress dialog box, click **Close**. This procedure is used to acquire the contents of the virtual memory or RAM. The actual file will not be used for analysis; however, another file will be supplied for use in Lab 11.2.

Figure 11-3 Obtain System Files

Course Technology/Cengage Learning

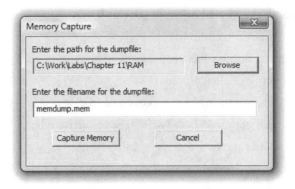

Figure 11-4   Capture virtual memory

Course Technology/Cengage Learning

12. Click the **File** tab, and click **Add Evidence Item**. In the Select Source dialog box, click **Contents of a Folder**, and click **Next**. Click **Browse** in the Select File dialog box, and locate the Virtual Memory evidence in the **C:\Work\Labs\Chapter 11\RAM** folder. Click **OK** in the Browse for Folder dialog box, and click **Finish** in the Select File dialog box.

13. Click the **+** symbol next to the RAM to expand the folder, and click the **C:\Work\ Labs\Chapter 11\RAM** object. Click the **Eyeglass** icon with the HEX text to look at the hex data.

14. Click the **memdump.mem** file in the File List window, and you see the contents of the virtual memory. Use the scroll bar to see all the data.

15. Leave FTK Imager open as you answer the review questions for this lab.

16. Close FTK Imager and any open windows on your desktop.

Review Questions

1. Where is the virtual memory of a computer contained?

   a. hard drive

   b. computer's BIOS

   c. computer's physical memory

   d. USB flash drive attached to the computer

2. What is the file name extension of the virtual memory?

   a. .doc

   b. .htm

   c. .mft

   d. .mem

3. What determines the virtual memory file size?

   a. hard drive size of the computer

   b. total time the computer has been turned on

   c. installed memory of the computer

   d. number of files stored in the computer's hard drive

4. The protected files captured by FTK Imager comprise what?

   a. the username and password of the registered user

   b. Windows Product Identification Value

   c. the deleted files held in the Recycle Bin

   d. the Windows registry files that control the computer's environment

5. FTK Imager provides how many options to capture the protected files?

   a. 2

   b. 1

   c. 4

   d. 6

Lab 11.2 Analyzing Virtual Memory Using Forensic Toolkit

Objectives

The virtual memory of a computer represents the contents of the physical RAM, and it may contain usable evidence related to a crime. Although the virtual memory is considered volatile in nature, it can be searched like any file using the FTK search tool after the memory has been captured and processed. The search feature in FTK can process large amounts of data in a short period, reducing the need to manually search each memory location. Forensics examiners can search terms, words, and applications that have been processed by the computer and the user during the commission of a crime. In addition, because virtual memory is temporary, existing only while the computer is running, examination of this evidence may be possible only before the computer is turned off to move it to a forensic lab. Therefore, it is critical to gather all the live evidence using tools that can acquire evidence without turning off the computer. FTK Imager Lite can be used to gather volatile data and save them to an external device for further processing before they will be lost forever. In this lab, you will process a virtual memory capture performed on a live computer.

After completing this lab, you will be able to:

- Add a virtual memory capture to FTK
- Search virtual memory for potential evidence

Materials Required

This lab requires the following:

- Windows Vista
- Forensic Toolkit (FTK) 1.81
- memdump.zip file

Estimated completion time: **25–30 minutes**

Activity

In this activity, you will add the memdump.mem file to FTK to search for evidence.

1. Copy the **memdump.zip** file located in the InChap11 folder located on the student data disk to the C:\Work\Labs\Chapter 11\RAM folder created in Lab 11.1.

2. Right-click the **memdump.zip** file located in the C:\Work\Labs\Chapter 11\RAM folder, and select **Extract All** from the context menu. Click **Extract** to unzip the compressed memdump.mem file, and close the window after the process completes.

3. Right-click the **FTK 1.81** icon on your desktop, and select **Run as administrator**. Click **Allow** in the User Account Control dialog box, and click **OK** in the CodeMeter.exe dialog box, if necessary.

4. Select **Start a new case** in the AccessData FTK Startup dialog box, if necessary, and click **OK**.

5. In the New Case dialog box, type **C11Proj2** in both the Case Number and Case Name boxes, and click **Next** six times until the Add Evidence to Case dialog box appears.

6. In the Add Evidence to Case dialog box, click **Add Evidence**, and select the **Contents of a Folder** button. Click **Continue** to navigate to the **C:\Work\Labs\Chapter 11\RAM\memdump** folder, and click **OK** in the Browse for Folder dialog box. Click **OK** in the Evidence Information dialog box, and click **Next** in the Add Evidence to Case dialog box. Click **Finish** in the Case Summary dialog box, and wait while FTK processes the evidence. This may take a few minutes to complete (see Figure 11-5).

Figure 11-5 Processing virtual memory

Course Technology/Cengage Learning

7. When FTK has finished processing the evidence, click the **Search** tab, and type **bank** in the Search Term box. Click the blue **Add** button, and note the search found 1620 Hits of the word **bank** in 35 Files in the Search Items box.

8. Type **search** in the Search Term box, click the blue **Add** button, and note that there are 6865 Hits in 41 Files. Also note that there are an additional 7601 instances where both **bank** and **search** are found together. Click the blue **View Cumulative Results** button, and click **OK** in the Filter Search Hits dialog box. In the Limit Search Hits dialog box, select **All hits**, check **Apply to all**, and click **OK**.

9. Click the + next to 7601 Hits in 35 Files to see all the instances where both words appear together. Click + next to the first 705 Hits location, and wait while FTK finds each location in memory.

10. Click the fourth hit (wait a few moments while FTK indexes the location), and use the scroll bar in the middle window to move down the memory location to see that John Smith used Bing in Internet Explorer to search for bank locations (see Figure 11-6). You may need to use the scroll bar slowly up and down to find this location.

11. Use the scroll bar, and move slowly down to see that John Smith also searched the http://www.yellowpages.com to find the Suntrust Bank Plantation location as well (see Figure 11-7).

12. Leave FTK open while you answer the review questions for this lab.

13. Close FTK, and click **No** in the FTK Exit Backup Confirmation dialog box.

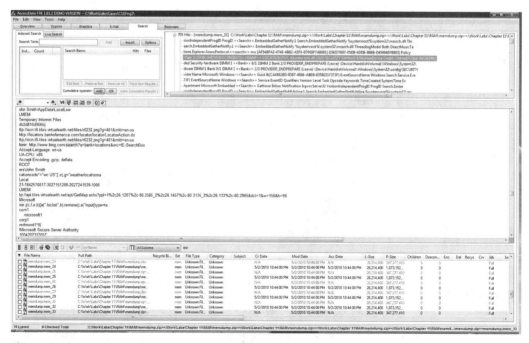

Figure 11-6 Search results

Course Technology/Cengage Learning

Figure 11-7   Additional results

Course Technology/Cengage Learning

Review Questions

1. What is the size of the memdump.mem file?

    a. 2,048,000 KB

    b. 2,048,000 KB

    c. 1,048,000 MB

    d. 339,139 KB

2. How many evidence items were processed by FTK?

    a. 42

    b. 83

    c. 1

    d. 82

3. How many hits are found searching using the word *password*?

    a. 1024

    b. 3084   → 1542

    c. 80

    d. 82

4. How many files are found searching the file extension *.doc*?

    a. 3084

    b. 80

    c. 38

    d. 1060

5. How many Cumulative Result Hits are found using both *password* and *.doc*?

    a. 3084

    b. 1993

    c. 80

    d. 74

Lab 11.3 Analyzing Windows Registry

Objectives

The Windows registry controls the operating system environment, and it is the central repository for all information regarding users, passwords, connected devices, and physical hardware. The data contained in the registry can be searched for evidence using the Microsoft Regedit tool or forensic tools such as AccessData's Registry Viewer. The Registry Viewer tool provides much more information than Regedit when viewing areas that contain user account names and their unique identity attributes. Windows does not display user information in a naturally readable fashion. Instead, every item listed in the registry that must be secure uses a 128-bit name called a globally unique ID (GUID). The GUIDs contain information that can be searched and linked to a particular user such as the last login or last storage device accessed. Therefore, information in the Windows registry can also reveal details regarding computer-related crimes. In this lab, you will examine registry hives (folders) for evidence using the Registry Viewer you installed in Chapter 1.

After completing this lab, you will be able to:

- Use a registry-viewing forensic tool
- Search for user account information

Materials Required

This lab requires the following:

- Windows Vista
- AccessData Registry Viewer
- Registry folder files

Estimated completion time: **30–40 minutes**

Activity

In this activity, you will add protected files to the Registry Viewer.

1. Right-click the **AccessData Registry Viewer** icon on the desktop, and select **Run as administrator**.

2. Click **Allow** in the User Account Control dialog box, and click **OK** in the CodeMeter. exe dialog box, if necessary. Click **OK** in the Registry Viewer dialog box warning that no dongle was found.

3. Maximize the window, if necessary, then click the **File** tab and click **Open**. Navigate to the InChap11 folder in the student data disk, and double-click the **Registry** folder.

4. Click the **SAM** file, and click **Open** in the dialog box.

5. Click the + symbol next to the SAM folder to expand it, and view the subfolders. Expand the **Domains, Account**, and **Users** folders to see the user account details.

6. Click the **000001F4** account registry key, and view the information on the Administrator account including the Last Logon Time (see Figure 11-8). Note the details in the lower-left Key Properties window. The unique System Identifier (SID) is listed as 500, indicating that this is the Windows built-in account created when the operating system was installed.

7. Click the **000001F5** folder, and note that the SID unique identifier for the Guest account is 501. This also indicates that the Guest account is a built-in account created during the Windows installation. Both Administrator and Guest are built-in accounts. Also note that this account is not disabled and has been used once along with the last access date.

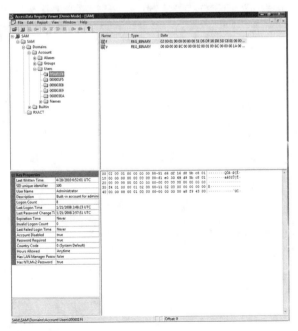

Figure 11-8   Administrator account details

Course Technology/Cengage Learning

8. Click the third, fourth, and fifth account folders, and answer Review Questions 1 through 3 below before proceeding to Step 9. The accounts with SID unique identifiers 1000 and higher were created by the administrator, and they are not built-in accounts. They belong to users who have accounts on the computer.

9. Click the **File** tab, click **Close**, and click **Yes** in the Registry Viewer dialog box to clear the current registry file from the Registry Viewer.

10. Click the **File** tab, and select **Open**. Double-click the **system** registry hive to load it into the Registry Viewer.

11. Expand the **ControlSet001, Enum**, and **STORAGE** folders. Expand the **Volume** folder located below the STORAGE folder to see all the storage devices that have been or are currently attached to the computer. This section includes both external and internal storage devices. Drag the edges of the window if necessary to view all the information.

12. Expand the **USBSTOR** folder to reveal all the USB devices that have been or are currently attached to this computer (see Figure 11-9). The entries here are only USB-type external storage devices. This information is useful for investigators looking for additional storage devices that may not be attached to the computer but were at one time.

13. Leave FTK open while you answer the last two review questions.

14. Click the **File** tab, and select **Exit**. Click **Yes** in the Registry Viewer dialog box to close the program.

Figure 11-9 Attached storage devices

Course Technology/Cengage Learning

Review Questions

1. What is the SID unique identifier associated with the John Smith use

    a. 1003

    b. 501

    c. 1000

    d. 1

2. What was the last time John Smith logged into the computer?

    a. 17:19:37 UTC

    b. 2:56:10 UTC

    c. 3:19:30 UTC

    d. He never logged into this computer

3. Besides Andrew, which other user has never logged into this computer?

    a. Administrator

    b. Guest

    c. William Smith

    d. John Smith

4. How many USB storage devices have been connected to this computer?

    a. 5

    b. 7

    c. 3

    d. 2

5. How many internal hard drives have been attached to this computer?

    a. 7

    b. 2

    c. 5

    d. 3

11

E-MAIL I...

Labs included in this chapter

158   Chapter 12   E-mail Investigations

Lab 12.1 Using Forensic
for Prelimin...

Objectives

E-mail evidence ca
enterprise e-ma
However, e
search fo
investi
e-m

Toolkit Imager to Search
ary E-mail Evidence

provide significant information involving computer-related crimes. Most systems that use storage servers can be imaged to recover forensic evidence. mail servers are often used throughout the day, and removing these servers to evidence can be disruptive to business operations. In most circumstances, forensics gators must first determine whether the files reside on the suspect's computer or the ail server before an image can be created. This search must be done first because imaging server storage disks can take several hours before the image can even be analyzed. Fortunately, Forensic Toolkit (FTK) Imager can be used to determine whether potential e-mail evidence exists on the user's computer before the investigator commits time to a detailed investigation. In this lab, you will perform an initial examination of a computer hard disk image to determine whether e-mail evidence may be present.

After completing this lab, you will be able to:

- Identify e-mail account structures
- Export a Microsoft Outlook .pst file

Materials Required

This lab requires the following:

- Windows Vista
- FTK Imager
- MS E-mail Files.E01 file

Estimated completion time: **20 minutes**

Activity

In this activity, you will add the MS E-mail Files.E01 file to FTK Imager and look for potential e-mail evidence.

1. Double-click the **FTK Imager** icon located on your desktop.

2. Click the **File** tab, and click **Add Evidence Item**.

3. Click **Image File** in the Select Source dialog box, and click **Next**.

4. Click the **Browse** button in the Select File dialog box, and navigate to the InChap12 folder located on the student data disk.

5. Click the **MS E-mail Files.E01** file, and click **Open**. In the Select File dialog box, click **Finish**.

6. Click the + symbol to expand each of the following folders:

- MS E-mail Files.E01
- NONAME [FAT12]

- [root]
- Identities
- {A9374354-3DF1-4AE3-99A1-589E67748E3A}
- Microsoft

7. Click the **Outlook** folder just below the [root] folder, and locate and click the **mailbox.pst** file. Click the **Eyeglass** icon with the text label to select the text reader in the lower-right window.

8. Drag the scroll bar on the right side of the window to look for e-mail messages, and ignore the Outlook ASCII formatting characters to look for readable text (see Figure 12-1).

9. After you examine the text entries, right-click the **mailbox.pst** file, and click **Export Files**. In the Browse for Folder dialog box, navigate to the C:\Work\Labs\ folder, and click **Make New Folder**. Type **Chapter 12**, press **Enter**, and click **OK** to copy the .pst file. Click **OK** in the Export Results dialog box. In Lab 12.2, you will examine a similar .pst file using FTK.

10. Click the **Outlook Express** folder below the Microsoft folder to examine the configured accounts (see Figure 12-2).

11. Click the **Hotmail Deleted Items.dbx** file to look for any messages. Unencrypted messages will be viewable in the text area. The first deleted message will be viewable in the text window. Use the scroll bar on the right side of the window to view any other deleted messages.

12. Click the **Sent Items.dbx** to see the first sent e-mail message in the text viewer (see Figure 12-3). Use the scroll bar on the right side of the window to view the second sent message.

Figure 12-1   E-mail text message

Course Technology/Cengage Learning

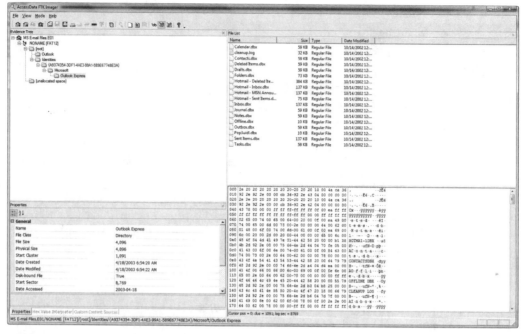

Figure 12-2 Outlook Express folder structure

Course Technology/Cengage Learning

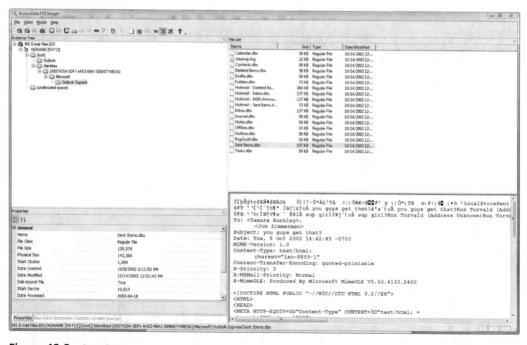

Figure 12-3 Sent items

Course Technology/Cengage Learning

13. Leave FTK Imager open while you answer the review questions for this lab.

14. Click the **File** tab, and select **Exit**.

Review Questions

1. What was the date the mailbox.pst file was last modified?

    a. 1/1/1980

    b. 4/18/2003

    c. 10/17/2002

    d. 12/12/2002

2. What is the file size of the Outlook Express folder?

    a. 4,096 KB

    b. 60,116 KB

    c. 21,000 MB

    d. 5,124 MB

3. What time were the Hotmail messages deleted?

    a. 7:05:34 AM

    b. 12:12:04 PM

    c. 12:51:42 PM

    d. 12:57:20 PM

4. How many messages were found in the Hotmail - Deleted Items.dbx mailbox?

    a. 2

    b. 1

    c. 3

    d. 4

5. What is the physical size of the Hotmail - Deleted Items mailbox?

    a. 392,816 KB

    b. 393,216 KB

    c. 392,816 MB

    d. 393,816 MB

12

Lab 12.2 Examining Exported Outlook E-mail Accounts

Objectives

Microsoft Outlook is a popular e-mail client software built into Microsoft Office or available as a stand-alone program. It is widely used because it supports many different types of e-mail server operation systems, and it allows the user to integrate contact information, calendar events, and e-mail messaging into one convenient program. Forensics investigators can often gather valuable evidence by searching Microsoft Outlook e-mail account information using forensic tools such as FTK. Microsoft Outlook provides an option to create a .pst backup file containing user information and messages. In this lab, you will add a .pst file to FTK and look for forensic information.

After completing this lab, you will be able to:

- Identify Microsoft Outlook backup files
- View a Microsoft Outlook .pst file in FTK

Materials Required

This lab requires the following:

- Windows Vista
- Forensic Toolkit (FTK) 1.81
- backup.pst file

Estimated completion time: **15–20 minutes**

Activity

In this activity, you will add a Microsoft Outlook backup.pst file to the FTK.

1. Right-click the **Forensic Toolkit 1.81** icon on your desktop, and click **Run as administrator**.

2. Click **Allow** in the User Account dialog box. Click **OK** in the CodeMeter.exe dialog box, if necessary.

3. Click **OK** in the AccessData FTK dialog box describing the 5000 maximum limit in the trial version of this software. This error will appear each time you start FTK.

4. Select **Start a new case** in the AccessData FTK Startup dialog box, if necessary, and click **OK**.

5. Type **C12Proj1** in both the Case Number and Case Name text boxes, and click **Next** six times until the Add Evidence to Case dialog box appears.

6. Click **Add Evidence** and **Individual File** in the Add Evidence to Case dialog box. Click **Continue**, and navigate to the InChap12 folder on the student data disk. Click the **backup.pst** file, and click **Open**.

7. Click **OK** in the Evidence Information dialog box. Click **Next**, and click **Finish** in the Case Summary dialog box to begin processing the e-mail .pst file. The file is now added to FTK (see Figure 12-4).

8. Click the **E-Mail** tab, and then click **List all descendants** to view all the e-mail files, mailboxes, and messages in the upper-right window.

9. Click the **+** symbol next to the backup.pst object and the Personal Folders folder. Click the **+** symbol next to the Top of Personal Folders folder to see the mailboxes associated with this e-mail account.

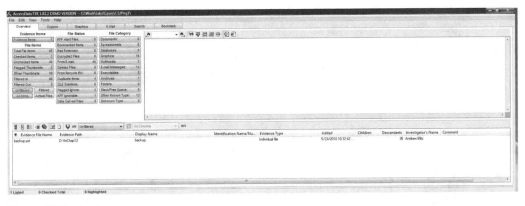

Figure 12-4   Backup.pst

Course Technology/Cengage Learning

10. Click the **Inbox** folder to see all messages received by this e-mail user. This view includes all the messages and any attachments associated with e-mails.

11. Click the first image attachment below Message0005. The image file sent as an attachment to Message0003 can be seen in the viewer, and the other image file attached to the message can be viewed (see Figure 12-5).

12. Click the **Sent Items** folder, and click Message0001; notice the three attached files that were sent by the user.

13. Click the **Pic_Safe1_Large** file attached to Message0001. This image was sent to the recipient by another person you discovered in Step 11 (see Figure 12-6).

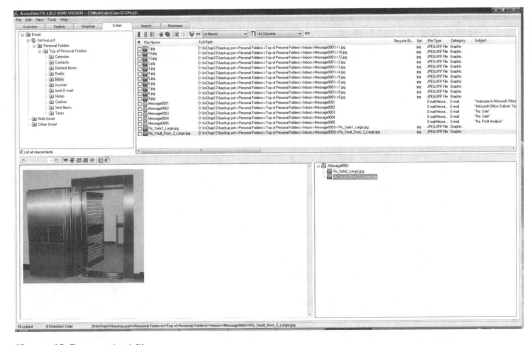

Figure 12-5   Attached files

Course Technology/Cengage Learning

Figure 12-6 Sent image

Course Technology/Cengage Learning

14. Leave FTK open as you answer the review questions for this lab.

15. Click the **File** tab, and click **Exit**. Click **No** in the FTK Exit Backup Confirmation dialog box.

Review Questions

1. What is the user account name associated with this backup.pst file?

   a. Jane Doe

   b. Mike Peters

   c. John Smith

   d. Bob Smith

2. To whom was the first e-mail message sent?

   a. John Smith

   b. Mike Peters

   c. Bob Smith

   d. Jane Doe

3. How many received messages contain attachments?

   a. 1

   b. 4

   c. 2

   d. 3

4. How many sent messages had attached images?

   a. 4

   b. 5

   c. 0

   d. 1

5. What is the name of the file sent by the e-mail user but not received by that same user as an attachment?

   a. Pic_Safe2_Large

   b. Pic_Safe1_Large

   c. Pic_Vault_Door_2_Large

   d. Message0001

Lab 12.3 Examining Hotmail Evidence

Objectives

Searching Internet e-mail can be problematic because of the various naming schemes, e-mail client file systems, and use of multiple e-mail storage servers that can be located anywhere in the world. In addition, forensics investigators need to associate an Internet e-mail message to a particular user, which is not easy because many people use an alias instead of a real name. Therefore, in many cases locally stored messages in user accounts can be critical to a case, and they must be traceable back to the user. The AccessData FTK provides extensive searching and sorting features useful to forensics investigators looking for potential evidence in local computers accessing client-based or Internet-based e-mail services. Internet-based e-mail services such as Hotmail typically store copies of e-mail messages in folders on the local computer by user account name in HTML-formatted files.

In this lab, you will add an e-mail image file to FTK that contains several e-mail accounts to examine the folder structures and look for potential evidence in the messages. After completing this lab, you will be able to:

- Add e-mail image files to FTK
- Recognize Hotmail e-mail folder structures

Materials Required

This lab requires the following:

- Windows Vista
- Forensic Toolkit (FTK) 1.81
- MS E-mail Files.E01

Estimated completion time: **15–20 minutes**

Activity

In this activity, you will add an e-mail image to FTK to search for evidence.

1. Right-click the **Forensic Toolkit 1.81** icon on your desktop, and click **Run as administrator**.

2. Click **Allow** in the User Account dialog box. Click **OK** in the CodeMeter.exe dialog box, if necessary.

3. Click **OK** in the AccessData FTK dialog box describing the 5000 maximum limit in the trial version of this software. This error will appear each time you start FTK.

4. Select **Start a new case** in the AccessData FTK Startup dialog box, if necessary, and click **OK**.

5. Type **C12Proj2** in both the Case Number and Case Name text boxes, and click **Next** six times until the Add Evidence to Case dialog box appears.

6. Click **Add Evidence**, and click **Acquired Image of Drive** in the Add Evidence to Case dialog box. Click **Continue**, and navigate to the InChap12 folder on the student data disk. Click the **MS E-mail Files.E01** file, and click **Open**.

7. In the Evidence Information dialog box, select **Pacific Time with Daylight Saving** in the Local Evidence Time Zone drop-down list. Click **OK** and click **Next**, followed by **Finish** in the Case Summary dialog box.

8. Close any virus scan alert messages if necessary (see Figure 12-7). There are no viruses present, but some antivirus software may detect files within this e-mail. Please disregard if necessary.

9. Click the **E-Mail** tab, and click **List all descendants** to view all the existing messages and deleted messages. There are multiple e-mail accounts in this image file. Use the scroll bar on the right side of the upper-right window to see all the files. The deleted messages contain a red X in the icon.

10. Right-click the deleted **Message0023**, and click **File Properties**. In the File Properties dialog box, click the **File Source Info** tab to see that this message was deleted but is not in the recycle bin (see Figure 12-8).

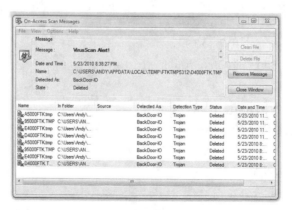

Figure 12-7   Possible virus files

Course Technology/Cengage Learning

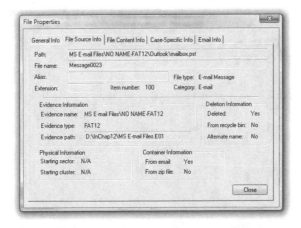

Figure 12-8 Deleted messages

Course Technology/Cengage Learning

11. Click the `File Content Info` tab to see the MD5 and SHA1 hash values associated with this deleted file.

12. Click the `E-mail Info` tab to see the E-mail Message Information, such as the Subject, Date, and sender of the message. Click `Close`. The details of the message can be viewed in the lower-left window.

13. Click the `Hotmail - Deleted Items.dbx` object to see the deleted Hotmail messages on this computer. These messages do not have the red X to indicate they were deleted; instead, they are moved to a deleted folder.

14. Click the `Overview` tab, and click the `Documents` bucket button under the File Category column to see the existing and deleted documents in this evidence.

15. Click the `Graphics` tab, and click the `List all descendants` check box to see all the recovered image files (see Figure 12-9).

16. Leave FTK open as you answer the review questions for this lab.

17. Click the `File` tab, and click `Exit`. Click `No` in the FTK Exit Backup Confirmation dialog box.

Review Questions

1. How many different graphics images are located in this e-mail evidence?

    a. 4

    b. 11

    c. 5

    d. 2

2. How many files have bad extensions?

    a. 2

    b. 4

    c. 11

    d. 5

Figure 12-9   Recovered graphics images

Course Technology/Cengage Learning

3. How many MS Word documents are located in this evidence?

    a. 18

    b. 1

    c. 5

    d. 3

4. How many deleted e-mail messages are located in this evidence?

    a. 36

    b. 18

    c. 63

    d. 87

5. What is the formatted file system in use in this evidence?

    a. FAT32

    b. FAT12

    c. NTFS

    d. HFS+

CELL PHONE AND MOBILE DEVICE FORENSICS

Labs included in this chapter

- Lab 13.1 Examining Cell Phone Storage Devices
- Lab 13.2 Using FTK Imager to View Extracted Phone Evidence
- Lab 13.3 Analyzing Cell Phone Evidence Using the Forensic Toolkit

Lab 13.1 Examining Cell Phone Storage Devices

Objectives

Most modern cell phones support removable memory storage devices known as MicroSD and MiniSD flash devices, and these devices can store up to 32 GB of data. An experienced computer forensics investigator will find that personal information, pictures, and organizer data can be obtained from the flash memory device. When creating images of cell phone data, it is advisable to remove any secondary storage devices and image them separately because flash memory is usually formatted in a readable file system.

Recovering cell phone information can be challenging because no formal standards exist on operating systems, and the file systems vary greatly between manufacturers. In this lab, you will use Forensic Toolkit (FTK) to process a forensically obtained image of a cell phone MicroSD storage device.

After completing this lab, you will be able to:

- Add cell phone removable storage device images to FTK
- Identify cell phone forensic data

Materials Required

This lab requires the following:

- Windows Vista
- Forensic Toolkit (FTK) 1.81
- C13Proj1.E01 file

Estimated completion time: **15–20 minutes**

Activity

In this activity, you will add a forensically extracted image of a cell phone MicroSD storage device to FTK for processing.

1. Right-click the **Forensic Toolkit 1.81** icon on your desktop, and click **Run as administrator.**

2. Click **Allow** in the User Account dialog box. Click **OK** in the CodeMeter.exe dialog box, if necessary.

3. Click **OK** in the AccessData FTK dialog box describing the 5000 maximum limit in the trial version of this software. This error will appear each time you start FTK.

4. Select **Start a new case** in the AccessData FTK Startup dialog box, if necessary, and click **OK.**

5. Type **C13Proj1** in both the Case Number and Case Name text boxes, and click **Next** six times until the Add Evidence to Case dialog box appears.

6. Click **Add Evidence**, and click **Acquired Image of Drive**, if necessary, in the Add Evidence to Case dialog box. Click **Continue**, and navigate to the InChap13 folder on the student data disk. Click the **C13Proj01.E01** file, and click **Open.**

7. In the Evidence Information dialog box under the Local Evidence Time Zone, choose **Eastern Time with Daylight Saving**. Click **OK**.

8. Click **Next** in the Add Evidence to Case dialog box, and click **Finish** in the Case Summary dialog box.

9. Click the **Explore** tab, and click the **List all descendants** check box. The contents of the SANVOL-FAT16 flash memory is listed in the upper-left window along with the deleted and existing graphics files stored on the MicroSD storage device (see Figure 13-1).

10. Click the deleted **02-10-07_1450** file in the upper window to view the recovered graphic in the viewer. Click the **02-10-07_1450.htm file** located in the bottom window, and Exif data listing the phone camera resolution will be displayed in the upper-right window. Each graphics file has corresponding Exif data located below it.

11. Drag the scroll bar on the right side of the upper-left window to see all the remaining files and folders located in the root of the MicroSD storage device. The folders located toward the bottom of the lower window contain the cell phone user's personal files.

12. Click the **Graphics** tab, and click the **List all descendants** check box to see all the graphics images stored on the storage device (see Figure 13-2). Click any graphic, and its associated file properties and hash values will be displayed in the highlighted area in the lower window. Drag the lower scroll bar to the right to see the file header and hash values.

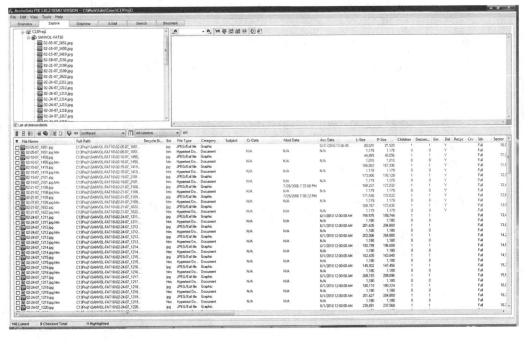

Figure 13-1   SANVOL-FAT16 files

Course Technology/Cengage Learning

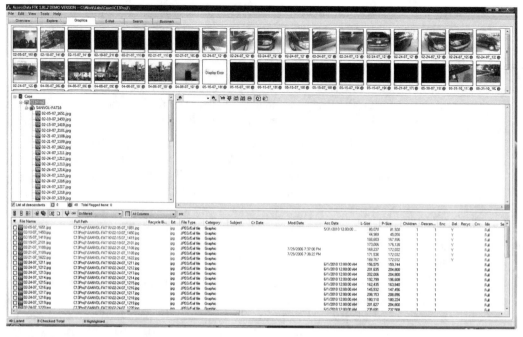

Figure 13-2 Graphics images

Course Technology/Cengage Learning

13. Click the **Overview** tab to see the buckets containing the files organized by their type. Click the **Unknown Type** bucket button to see all the deleted files that could not be recovered or viewed (see Figure 13-3).

14. Leave FTK open while you answer the review questions for this lab.

15. Click the **File** tab, and click **Exit**. Click **No** in the FTK Exit Backup Confirmation dialog box to close FTK.

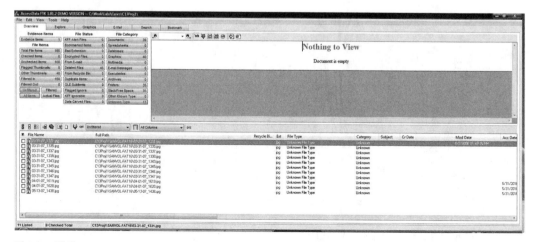

Figure 13-3 Unknown files

Course Technology/Cengage Learning

Review Questions

1. What is the total number of file items found on this storage device?

   a. 40

   b. 46

   c. 160

   d. 4

2. How many folders are located on this storage device?

   a. 11

   b. 40

   c. 160

   d. 35

3. What is the formatted file system in use on this storage device?

   a. NTFS

   b. FAT32

   c. FAT16

   d. HPF+

4. What is the resolution of the camera built into the cell phone?

   a. cannot be determined from the evidence

   b. 3.0 MP (megapixel)

   c. 4.0 MP

   d. 1.3 MP

5. What information can be found in the Documents bucket under the File Category column?

   a. exif data for the graphics images

   b. MS Word documents

   c. file hash values

   d. graphics images

Lab 13.2 Using FTK Imager to View Extracted Phone Evidence

Objectives

Computer forensics investigators must be able to extract locally stored data in cell phones because service providers do not have access to the personal information. The imaging process requires both hardware and software tools to successfully connect a forensic recovery computer to the large variety of cell phone models in use. Special-purpose USB adaptors provide the electrical connections that allow AccessData's Mobile Phone Examiner (MPE) to read the stored data. AccessData's MPE creates .ad1-formatted images that can be processed by FTK or FTK Imager to recover potential forensic evidence. Because of the large variations among cell phone file systems, recovering data may be more efficient using FTK Imager because it provides a faster analysis of resident memory data and FTK can be used as a secondary tool to document the investigation. In this lab, you will process the MPE image of a LG 6000 cell phone to look for potential evidence.

After completing this lab, you will be able to:

- Add forensic cell phone data to FTK Imager
- Describe a typical cell phone file format

Materials Required

This lab requires the following:

- Windows Vista
- FTK Imager
- LG_6000_4d76e052.ad1 file

Estimated completion time: **15–20 minutes**

Activity

In this activity, you will add the LG_6000_4d76e052.ad1 cell phone data image to FTK Imager to look for potential evidence.

1. Double-click the **FTK Imager** icon located on your desktop.

2. Click the **File** tab, and click **Add Evidence Item**.

3. Click **Image File** in the Select Source dialog box, and click **Next**.

4. Click the **Browse** button in the Select File dialog box, and navigate to the InChap13 folder located on the student data disk.

5. Click the **LG_6000_4d76e052.ad1** file, and click **Open**. In the Select File dialog box, click **Finish**.

6. Click the + symbol next to the **LG_6000_4d76e052.ad1** icon to expand it. Expand the **External-File-System [AD1]** connector object and the following folders: **LG VX6000**, **LG VX6000**, and **Phonebook**.

7. Click the **Last dialed numbers** folder to view the last numbers stored in the phone's internal memory (see Figure 13-4). The numbers are displayed in the upper-right window. Use the scroll bar on the right side to view all the numbers, if necessary.

8. Click the **Received calls** folder to see all the inbound calls to the phone. The time and date are not available in this capture, but they can be obtained from the service provider.

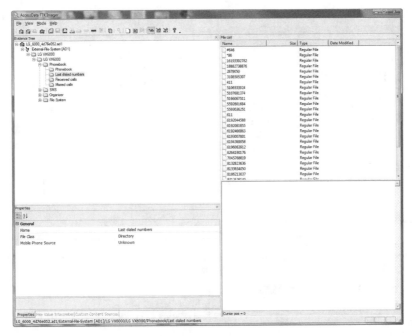

Figure 13-4   Last dialed numbers

Course Technology/Cengage Learning

9. Click the **Missed calls** folder to see all the inbound calls to the phone that were not answered.

10. Click the + symbol next to the **File System** folder to expand it and view the sub-folders. Click the **sms** folder below the File System folder to view any text messages sent to the phone.

11. Click the **mediacan000.dat** file, and click on the **TEXT Eyeglass** icon on the tool bar to view the text message sent to the phone in the lower-right window (see Figure 13-5).

12. Click the **pim** folder, and click the **outgoing_log.dat** file to see the outgoing call log and the caller ID name. Use the scroll bar on the right side of the lower window to see all the numbers and their associated names. Disregard the ASCII characters to the left of the numbers because they are used by the phone database.

13. Click the **missed_log.dat** file to see the numbers and names of calls that were not answered on the phone.

14. Click the **incoming_log.dat** file to see the inbound call list (see Figure 13-6).

15. Click the **Eyeglass** icon on the tool bar, and click the **cam** folder to look for graphics images taken by the cell phone camera. Click each picture to see it in the viewer.

16. Leave FTK Imager open as you answer the review questions for this lab.

17. Click the **File** tab, and select **Exit** to close FTK Imager.

Figure 13-5 SMS text message

Course Technology/Cengage Learning

Figure 13-6 Inbound call list

Course Technology/Cengage Learning

Review Questions

1. How many valid phone numbers wer

   a. 24

   b. 26

   c. It cannot be determined based on

   d. There were no numbers dialed.

2. How many inbound calls could not

   a. 6

   b. 4

   c. 23

   d. 30

3. How many different missed calls or

   a. 7

   b. 5

   c. 26

   d. 4

4. How many camera pictures were found on this cell phone?

   a. 6

   b. 5

   c. 10

   d. 0

5. How many dialed calls were local numbers (not long distance)?

   a. 0

   b. 1

   c. 23

   d. 5

Lab 13.3 Analyzing Cell Phone Evidence Using the Forensic Toolkit

Objectives

Modern cell phones can contain multimedia and text files such as pictures, movies, and documents that may be valuable to an investigation. Because there are no worldwide cell phone standards used to store electronic data, forensic tools must be able to read the various file formats to locate information. Although FTK Imager is useful in locating most cell phone data, it lacks reporting, data-carving, and powerful search capabilities. Fortunately,

Chapter 13 Cell Phone and Mobile D

178

FTK includes file viewers to
to locate and document
5300 MPE image with
After completing

• Add a fore
• Look f

Mat
Th

process graphics and other multimedia files, and it can be used
potential cell phone evidence. In this lab, you will process a Nokia
FTK to look for forensic evidence.
this lab, you will be able to:

sically captured cell phone image to the FTK

or SMS text messages

rials Required

s lab requires the following:

- Windows Vista
- Forensic Toolkit (FTK) 1.81
- Nokia_5300.ad1 file

Estimated completion time: **30–40 minutes**

Activity

In this activity, you will add the Nokia_5300.ad1 image to FTK to search for forensic evidence in the cell phone.

1. Right-click the **Forensic Toolkit 1.81** icon on your desktop, and click **Run as administrator**.

2. Click **Allow** in the User Account dialog box. Click **OK** in the CodeMeter.exe dialog box, if necessary.

3. Click **OK** in the AccessData FTK dialog box describing the 5000 maximum limit in the trial version of this software. This error will appear each time you start FTK.

4. Select **Start a new case** in the AccessData FTK Startup dialog box, if necessary, and click **OK**.

5. Type **C13Proj3** in both the Case Number and Case Name text boxes, and click **Next** six times until the Add Evidence to Case dialog box appears.

6. Click **Add Evidence**, and click **Acquired Image of Drive**, if necessary, in the Add Evidence to Case dialog box. Click **Continue**, and navigate to the InChap13 folder on the student data disk. Click the **Nokia_5300.ad1** file, and click **Open**.

7. In the Evidence Information dialog box, select **Mountain Time with Daylight Saving** in the Local Evidence Time Zone drop-down list. Click **OK** and click **Next**, followed by **Finish** in the Case Summary dialog box.

8. Click the **Explore** tab, and click the **List all descendants** check box to see all the recoverable files located on the Nokia 5300 cell phone (see Figure 13-7). The files are listed in alphabetical order by file name, and they need to be sorted to group similar files together.

9. Click the **Full Path** column heading in the lower window. Drag the scroll bar on the right side of the window down until you see the SMS folder and the Inbox folder just below it. Each message can be seen in alphabetical order just below the Inbox folder.

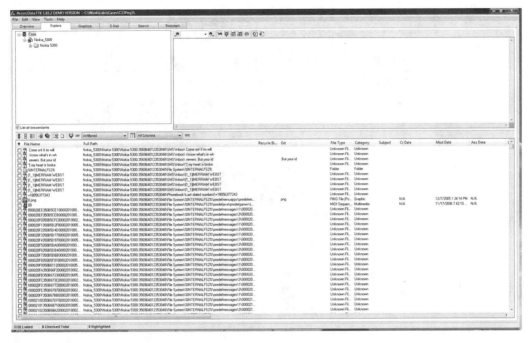

Figure 13-7   Recovered files

Course Technology/Cengage Learning

10. Click the **Graphics** tab, and click the **List all descendants** check box to see all the graphics files on the cell phone.

11. Click the **Ext** column heading in the lower window to sort the files by file extension. Drag the scroll bar down until you see the Image000 file, and click it to see the JPEG image in the viewer (see Figure 13-8).

12. Click the **Search** tab, and click the **Live Search** tab. Type **url** in the Search Term box, and click **Add**.

13. Click the blue **Search** button, and click **OK** to look for any URLs searched via the cell phone's web browser. After the Live Search has completed, click the **View Results** button in the Live Search Progress dialog box.

14. Click the **Search Performed** with the date and time stamp link at the upper-right top window. All the files associated with Internet downloads will be viewable in the lower window.

15. Drag the scroll bar down until you see the Test000.3gp file; right-click it, and select **Launch Associated Program**. The movie file will be viewable if you have Real Player or QuickTime installed in your computer. If you do not have either software, download one from the Internet, and after it is installed, repeat the process to view the recovered video (see Figure 13-9).

16. Close the Real Player or QuickTime application, and leave FTK open as you answer the review questions for this lab.

17. Click the **File** tab, and select **Exit**. Click **No** in the FTK Exit Backup Confirmation dialog box to close FTK.

Figure 13-8 Graphics image

Course Technology/Cengage Learning

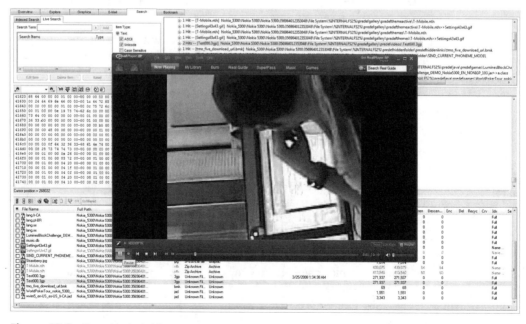

Figure 13-9 Downloaded video

Course Technology/Cengage Learning

Review Questions

1. When was the video downloaded to the cell phone?

   a. 1/2/2007 at 1:52 PM

   b. 3/13/2007 at 5:03 PM

   c. 3/25/2008 at 1:34 AM

   d. 7/31/2006 at 1:29 PM

2. What is the total number of File Items recovered during this forensic search?

   a. 3330

   b. 385

   c. 1151

   d. 1717

3. How many flash files (.swf) were found on this cell phone?

   a. 41

   b. 16

   c. 3

   d. 6

4. How many JPEG files were recovered in this cell phone image?

   a. 29

   b. 41

   c. 385

   d. 63

5. How many items are duplicate files?

   a. 63

   b. 178

   c. 41

   d. 385

13

REPORT WRITING FOR HIGH-TECH INVESTIGATIONS

Labs included in this chapter

- Lab 14.1 Using FTK Imager to Document Case Evidence
- Lab 14.2 Using ProDiscover to Create a Report
- Lab 14.3 Using the Forensic Toolkit to Create a Report

Lab 14.1 Using FTK Imager to Document Case Evidence

Objectives

In previous labs you learned that forensics examiners typically use many tools to look for evidence and then compare the results in an effort to perform a thorough examination. We have used FTK Imager to look for preliminary evidence and then export the results for further analysis. Although FTK Imager does not provide detailed reports on recovered data, it does provide file and hash information useful to forensics investigators. In this lab, you will add the Firestarter hard disk image to FTK Imager and export file names, directory lists, and hash signatures to document the recovered evidence.

After completing this lab, you will be able to:

- Use FTK Imager to look for forensic evidence
- Export files, folders, and hash signature information

Materials Required

This lab requires the following:

- Windows Vista with Office 2003 or 2007
- FTK Imager
- Firestarter.zip

Estimated completion time: **15–20 minutes**

Activity

In this activity, you will examine the Firestarter.dd file using FTK Imager.

1. Navigate to the InChap14 folder on your student data disk, right-click the **Firestarter. zip** file, and select **Extract All**.

2. Click **Browse** in the Extract Compressed (Zipped) Folders dialog box, navigate to the **C:\Work\Labs\Evidence** folder, click **OK** in the Select a Destination dialog box, and click **Extract**.

3. Create a **Chapter 14** folder in the C:\Work\Labs folder.

4. Double-click the **FTK Imager** icon located on your desktop.

5. Click the **File** tab, and click **Add Evidence Item**.

6. Click **Image File** in the Select Source dialog box, and click **Next**.

7. Click the **Browse** button in the Select File dialog box, navigate to the **C:\Work\Labs\ Evidence** folder, select the **Firestarter.dd** file, and click **Open**. Click **Finish** in the Select File dialog box to add the image to FTK Imager.

8. Click the + symbols to expand the **Firestarter.dd, FIRESTARTER [FAT32]**, and **[root]** icons (see Figure 14-1).

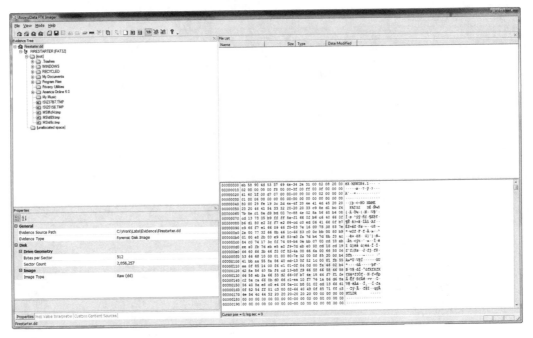

Figure 14-1   Firestarter image

Course Technology/Cengage Learning

9. Right-click the **Firestarter.dd** icon, and select **Export Directory Listing**.

10. Navigate to the **C:\Work\Labs\Chapter 14** folder, type **C14Proj1** in the File Name text box, click **Save**, and click **Close** in the Creating Directory Listing [100%] dialog box to export the list of files.

11. Right-click the **FIRESTARTER [FAT32]** icon, select **Export File Hash List**, navigate to the **C:\Work\Labs\Chapter 14** folder if necessary, type **firestarter file hashes** in the File Name text box, and click **Save** in the Save As dialog box. This may take a few minutes depending on your computer's CPU speed.

12. In Windows Explorer, double-click on the **C14Proj1.csv** file in the C:\Work\Labs\ Chapter 14 folder to see the list of exported file names, the file paths on the disk, and other file attributes displayed in MS Excel. Drag column headers to the right to increase the column widths and see the details (see Figure 14-2).

13. Click the **Minimize** button in the upper-right corner of the window to minimize the file to the task bar.

14. Double-click the **firestarter file hashes.csv** file in the C:\Work\Labs\Chapter 14 folder.

15. Increase the width of the MD5 and SHA1 columns to view the entire hash signatures of the files located on the image (see Figure 14-3).

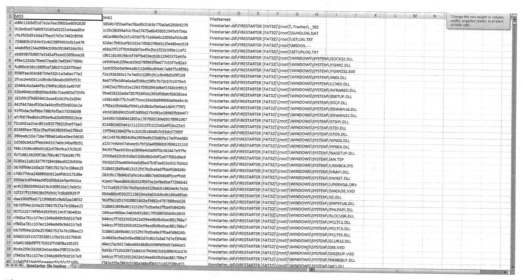

Figure 14-2 Directory listing

Course Technology/Cengage Learning

Figure 14-3 File hashes

Course Technology/Cengage Learning

16. Leave the MS Excel files and FTK Imager open as you answer the review questions for this lab.

17. Close the two MS Excel files, click **No** in the Microsoft Office Excel dialog boxes, and close MS Excel.

18. Click the **File** tab, and select **Exit** to close FTK Imager.

Review Questions

1. What is the volume serial number of the Firestarter hard disk image?

   a. FIRESTARTER

   b. 2,056,257

   c. 2D3C-19FE

   d. cannot be determined in the evidence

2. What date was the Windows file system in this image last accessed?

   a. 3/22/2009

   b. 7/23/2004

   c. 7/24/2004

   d. 3/13/2007

3. What deleted MS Office file was found on the Firestarter hard disk image?

   a. !NFO2

   b. !C0.TXT

   c. Dc3.XLS

   d. DC3.doc

4. What is the size of the FAT folders?

   a. 4096

   b. 1536

   c. 15872

   d. 1027584

5. What two files have the same file MD5 and SHA1 hashes?

   a. FAT1, FAT2

   b. house3, housefire

   c. lgfire1, pyr1

   d. firestarter3.WMV, firestarter3.zip

14

Lab 14.2 Using ProDiscover to Create a Report

Objectives

ProDiscover provides basic report tools that are useful to forensics investigators performing an initial search of recovered evidence. In this lab, you will add the firestarter.dd image to ProDiscover and use the reporting tools to document the evidence.

After completing this lab, you will be able to:

- Use ProDiscover to analyze forensic evidence
- Use the ProDiscover reporting tools to document recovered evidence

Materials Required

This lab requires the following:

- Windows Vista with Office 2003 or 2007 installed
- ProDiscover
- Completion of Lab 14.1
- Firestarter.dd file

Estimated completion time: **30–40 minutes**

Activity

In this activity, you will add the Firestarter.dd image to ProDiscover.

1. Double-click the **ProDiscover Basic** icon located on your desktop.

2. Click the **New Project** icon on the tool bar, and type **C14Proj2** in both the Project Number and Project File Name text boxes in the New Project dialog box. Type **Arson Case** in the Description text box, and click **OK** in the New Project dialog box.

3. Click the **Action** tab, click **dd** from the drop-down menu, and then click **Image File**.

4. In the Open dialog box, navigate to the **C:\Work\Labs\Evidence\Firestarter. dd** file you extracted in Lab 14.1, click it, and click **Open**.

5. Click the **+** symbol next to the **Images** icon located under the Cluster View folder, and click the **C:\Work\Labs\Evidence\Firestarter.dd** icon to examine the hard disk file system (see Figure 14-4). Note the MSWIN4.1 operating system indicating this is a Windows 98 hard disk partition.

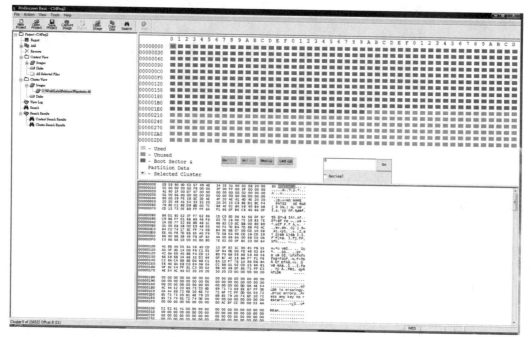

Figure 14-4 Windows 98 partition

Course Technology/Cengage Learning

6. Click the + symbol next to the **Images** icon located under the Content View folder, and also click the `C:\Work\Labs\Evidence\Firestarter.dd` icon to see the Windows 98 operating system folders.

7. Click the + symbol next to the C:\Work\Labs\Evidence\Firestarter.dd icon to expand the list of folders in the left tree window, and click the **My Documents** folder to highlight it. Click the **View** tab, and select **Gallery View** to see the files, folders, and any documents or images in the My Documents folder. Deleted files and folders are indicated by the red X over the icon.

8. In the left window, click the + symbol next to the My Documents to expand the folder, and click the first deleted folder under the My Documents folder (it is named %OOLPIX) to see the deleted images of fires. Click the check box to the lower left of the first picture in the Gallery window, and type **recent undetermined fires** in the Investigator Comments text box in the Add Comment dialog box (see Figure 14-5). Click **OK** to bookmark the image; a check mark should appear in the box.

9. Double-click the next deleted image, type **recent undetermined fire** in the Investigators Comments text box in the Add Comment dialog box, and click **OK**. Repeat this process for all the deleted images. After you bookmark the last image, verify all the check boxes are selected.

10. Click the **Business** folder under the My Documents folder, and double-click the **CV.DOC** file icon in the upper-right window to view the file in MS Word. Bookmark the file using the process above, and type **Casey CV** in the Investigator Comments text box. Click **OK** in the Add Comment dialog box.

11. Click the **Data** folder to see the files inside it, and examine the deleted MS Excel file by double-clicking it to see the list of dates and times of recent fires. Bookmark this file, and type **list of dates and times of fires** in the Investigator Comments text box. Click **OK** in the Add Comment dialog box.

12. Click the **Lumbermill** folder, and bookmark the images because they depict images of lumber mills that were later found on fire. Type **future fires** in the Investigator Comments text box.

13. Click the deleted **New** folder, and locate the .htm file that contains the shopping cart containing the police/fire scanner recovered at the scene of one of the fires. Bookmark this file as **scanner evidence recovered at a fire scene**.

14

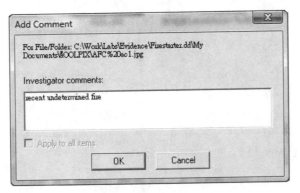

Figure 14-5   Evidence images

Course Technology/Cengage Learning

14. Click the deleted **Plans** folder, and bookmark the two deleted password-protected files named Burninator because this name is significant in an arson case. Perhaps it is an alias the suspect uses. Bookmark these files as **Burninator password protected documents**.

15. Click the **Pleasure** folder, and bookmark each of the fire images as **recent undetermined fires**.

16. Click the **WALMART** folder, and bookmark the images as **recent Wal-Mart fires**.

17. Click the **View** tab, and select **Report** to view the case report (see Figure 14-6).

18. Leave ProDiscover open as you answer the review questions for this lab.

19. Click the **File** tab, and select **Exit** to close ProDiscover. Click **No** in the ProDiscover dialog box.

Review Questions

1. What is the number of files located as Evidence of Interest?

    a. 60

    b. 25

    c. 40

    d. 33

Figure 14-6   ProDiscover report

Course Technology/Cengage Learning

2. What is the volume serial number of this hard drive evidence?

   a. NO NAME

   b. 256526

   c. 2D3C-19FE

   d. 512

3. How many hidden sectors were located on this evidence?

   a. 512

   b. 63

   c. 256526

   d. 60

4. How many deleted folders were located in the root of this evidence?

   a. 5

   b. 6

   c. 25

   d. 38

5. What is the file system in use on this hard drive evidence?

   a. NTFS

   b. FAT32

   c. FAT16

   d. MSWIN4.1

Lab 14.3 Using the Forensic Toolkit to Create a Report

Objectives

The Forensic Toolkit (FTK) provides detailed search and reporting tools. In Lab 14.2, you examined the Firstarter.dd file using ProDiscover and located the names Casey and Burninator in the forensic image. In this lab, you will add the Firestarter.dd image to FTK to search for additional evidence to build your case and summarize your findings in the case report.

After completing this lab, you will be able to:

- Examine evidence using search tools
- Create a case report in FTK

Materials Required

This lab requires the following:

- Windows Vista
- Forensic Toolkit (FTK) 1.81
- Successful completion of Lab 14.1
- Firestarter.dd file

Estimated completion time: **30–40 minutes**

Activity

In this activity, you will use a protocol analyzer to capture FTP traffic and analyze the results.

1. Right-click the **Forensic Toolkit 1.81** icon on your desktop, and click **Run as administrator**.

2. Click **Allow** in the User Account dialog box. Click **OK** in the CodeMeter.exe dialog box, if necessary.

3. Click **OK** in the AccessData FTK dialog box describing the 5000 maximum limit in the trial version of this software. This error will appear each time you start FTK.

4. Select **Start a new case** in the AccessData FTK Startup dialog box, if necessary, and click **OK**.

5. Type **C14Proj3** in both the Case Number and Case Name text boxes, and click **Next** six times until the Add Evidence to Case dialog box appears.

6. Click **Add Evidence**, and click **Acquired Image of Drive** if necessary in the Add Evidence to Case dialog box. Click **Continue**, and navigate to the **C:\Work\Labs\ Evidence\Firestarter.dd** file you extracted in Lab 14.1. Click the **Firestarter. dd** file, and click **Open**.

7. Select **Eastern Time with Daylight Saving** in the Local Evidence Time Zone text box, type **Arson Case** in the Comment text box, and click **OK** in the Evidence Information dialog box.

8. Click **Next** in the Add Evidence to Case dialog box, and click **Finish** in the Case Summary dialog box. This may take a few minutes to complete.

9. Click **OK** in the FTK Demo Version dialog box. This warning will not affect the lab project. The Overview tab will display file statistics of the recovered hard disk image (see Figure 14-7).

10. Click the **Explore** tab, and click the **List all descendants** check box to see all the recovered files on the Windows 98 hard disk image. Note the root file structure is similar to the ProDiscover image (see Figure 14-5 in Lab 14.2).

11. Click the **Graphics** tab, and check the **List all descendants** check box to see all the recovered images on this evidence.

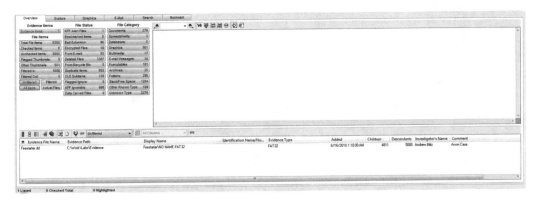

Figure 14-7 Case overview

Course Technology/Cengage Learning

12. Use the scroll bar on the right side of the top window to see all images, click the red circle to turn it into a green box, and bookmark the image. Look for images related to fires, lumber yards, Wal-Mart stores, firemen, and any other images containing **fire** in the name or picture. You can enlarge each image in the viewer to find them all and bookmark them using the process described above.

13. Right-click any flagged green image, select **Export Flagged Green Items**, navigate to the **C:\Work\Labs\Chapter 14** folder in the Destination Path text box, check the **Append appropriate extension to the file name if bad/absent** check box, and click **OK** in the Export Flagged Green Files dialog box. Click **OK** in the Export Files dialog box when complete. The files will be exported to the Chapter 14 folder.

14. Scroll to the top of the list of images, and hold the **Control** key as you select each green flagged image. Right-click any selected image, and click **Create Bookmark**.

15. Type **Fires** in the Bookmark Name text box and **Arson Evidence** in the Bookmark Comment text box. Check the **Include in report** check box; click the **All highlighted items** button, if necessary; and click **OK** in the Create New Bookmark dialog box.

16. Click the **Search** tab, type **casey** in the Search Term text box, and click the **Options** button. In the Search Options dialog box, select the **Phonic** and **Fuzzy** check boxes to find all the possible spellings of **casey**, and click **OK**. Click **Add** to add the word to the Search Items.

17. Type **burninator** in the Search Term text box, and click **Add**. Type **Kasey** in the Search Term dialog box, and click **Add**. Click the **OR** button, click the **View Cumulative Results** button, and click **OK** in the Filter Search Hits dialog box. Click **OK** three times in the Limit Search Hits dialog box.

18. Click the + symbol next to the 2969 Hits in 335 Files list to display all the files related to the search terms.

14

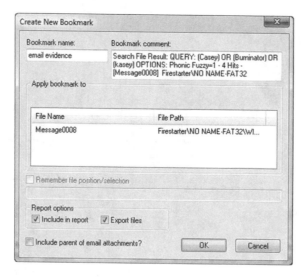

Figure 14-8 Bookmark e-mail evidence

Course Technology/Cengage Learning

19. Scroll down to and click **4 Hits - [Message0008]** to see a sent e-mail from P. Kasey containing incriminating evidence. Right-click the highlighted file, and select **Bookmark Search File Result**. Type **email evidence** in the Bookmark name, check the **Include in report** check box, and check the **Export files** (see Figure 14-8).

20. Click the **File** tab, select **Report Wizard**, click **Next** seven times, and click **Finish** in the FTK Report Wizard - Report Location dialog box. Click **Yes** in the Report Wizard dialog box to view the report (see Figure 14-9).

21. Leave FTK and the report open while you answer the review questions for this lab.

22. Click the **File** tab, and select **Exit**. Click **No** in the FTK Exit Backup Confirmation dialog box. Close the FTK Case Report.

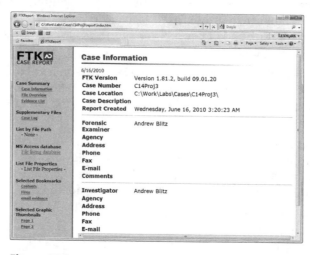

Figure 14.9 Case report

Course Technology/Cengage Learning

Review Questions

1. How many deleted folders were located in the root of this evidence?

    a. 5

    b. 6

    c. 25

    d. 38

2. How many Arson Evidence image files are listed under the Fires link in the report?

    a. 60

    b. 501

    c. 61

    d. 17

3. Where can all the procedures performed on this evidence be found in the report?

    a. under the Case Information link

    b. File Overview link

    c. Case Log link

    d. Contents link

4. How many e-mail messages were recovered in this evidence?

    a. 30

    b. 55

    c. 67

    d. 61

5. How many deleted files were recovered from the Recycle Bin?

    a. 3387

    b. 0

    c. 96

    d. 18

14

ADVANCED FORENSICS

Lab included in this chapter

- Lab 15.1 Using the Tool Suite to Search for Information

Lab 15.1 Using the Tool Suite to Search for Information

Objectives

Forensic evidence may be present in many different file formats within computer hard drives. The Windows registry stores information locally on the computer. The information includes items such as user names, passwords, time stamp details, and other related permissions and policies. Establishing a timeline around criminal activity can often be based on the computer-generated files found in the registry and the actual users logged into the computer. In addition, cyber criminals often maintain multiple e-mail accounts or types within the same computer to minimize detection and provide alternate aliases. Therefore, computer forensics investigators must be able to locate potential evidence in computer programs, data files, and web-based software—that is, in locations that may not be easily discovered. In this lab, you will examine a Windows forensic image to look for potential evidence using the Forensic Toolkit (FTK) text search features and the Registry Viewer.

After completing this lab, you will be able to:

- Use the Registry Viewer to locate user account information
- Use the Search features to locate information within the evidence

Materials Required

This lab requires the following:

- Windows Vista
- Forensic Toolkit (FTK) 1.81
- precious.zip file

Estimated completion time: **30 minutes**

Activity

In this activity, you will add the precious.001 image to FTK to examine its advanced forensic recovery and search features.

1. Create a **Chapter 15** folder in your C:\Work\Labs folder.

2. Locate the precious.zip folder in the InChap15 folder on the student data disk, right-click it, and select **Extract All**.

3. In the Extract Compressed (Zipped) Folders dialog box, uncheck the **Show extracted files when complete** box, click **Browse**, navigate to the **C:\Work\Labs\Chapter 15** folder, and click **OK** in the Select a Destination dialog box.

4. Click **Extract** in the Extract Compressed (Zipped) Folders dialog box to extract the precious.001 image to the Chapter 15 folder.

5. Right-click the **Forensic Toolkit 1.81** icon on your desktop, and click **Run as administrator**.

6. Click **Allow** in the User Account dialog box. Click **OK** in the CodeMeter.exe dialog box, if necessary.

7. Click **OK** in the AccessData FTK dialog box describing the 5000 maximum limit in the trial version of this software. This error will appear each time you start FTK.

8. Select **Start a new case** in the AccessData FTK Startup dialog box, if necessary, and click **OK**.

9. Type **C15Proj1** in both the Case Number and Case Name text boxes, click **Next** three times until the Processes to Perform dialog box appears, and check both the **Data Carve** and **Registry Reports** check boxes (see Figure 15-1). In the Processes to Perform dialog box, click **Next** three times.

10. Click **Add Evidence**, and select **Acquired Image of Drive**, if necessary, in the Add Evidence to Case dialog box. Click **Continue**; in the Look In: text box, navigate to the C:\Work\Labs\Chapter 15 folder, click the **precious.001** file, and click **Open**.

11. In the Evidence Information dialog box, type **Precious Evidence Image** in the Comment text box, and click **OK**.

12. Click **Next** in the Add Evidence to Case dialog box, and click **Finish** in the Case Summary dialog box to begin processing the image. This may take several minutes to complete.

13. The Overview tab will be displayed along with the recovered files in their respective descriptive buckets (see Figure 15-2). Click the **File** tab, and select **Registry Viewer** from the context menu.

14. In the Registry File List dialog box, select the **precious\Part_1\The Precious-NTFS\Windows\system32\config\Sam** registry file in the Select a registry file to view: list, and click **View file** to launch the Registry Viewer application.

Figure 15-1   Processes to Perform dialog box

Course Technology/Cengage Learning

Figure 15-2   Precious image

Course Technology/Cengage Learning

15. Click **OK** in the Registry Viewer dialog box warning "No dongle found" (this is normal), and click **OK** in the CodeMeter.exe dialog box, if necessary. Click the + symbols next to the **SAM, Domains, Account**, and **Users** folders to expand them and view the user accounts located on this computer hard drive image. Click each **Users** folder, and look for the user name associated with each SAM password account folder.

16. Click the **000003EC** folder to locate the Frodo Baggins user name in the Key Properties window along with the last logon time information. Use the scroll bar to view all the account information, including the number of times this user has logged into this computer (see Figure 15-3). Write this user name down on a piece of paper as you prepare a list of user names to search.

17. Click each of the user accounts below the 000003EC folder, and add any user names to the list in Step 16 that have logged into this computer image at least once.

18. Close the Registry Viewer window, and select **Yes** in the Registry Viewer dialog box.

Figure 15-3   SAM user account information

Course Technology/Cengage Learning

19. In the Registry File List dialog box, select the **precious\Part_1\The Precious-NTFS\Windows\system32\config\system** registry file, click **View file**, and click **OK** in the Registry Viewer dialog box to open the system registry file in the Registry Viewer.

20. Click the **+** symbols next to the **ControlSet001**, **Enum**, and **USBSTOR** folders to expand them and see a list of all the USB storage devices that have been attached to this computer. This information might be useful in looking for additional potential evidence that may exist on removable USB storage devices located at the seizure site. Minimize the Registry Viewer and Registry File List windows.

21. Click the **E-Mail** tab, and click the **+** symbol next to the **Email** icon if necessary to see all the e-mail folders associated with accounts on this computer image (see Figure 15-4). The e-mail accounts are grouped by application type, such as .dbx folders for Outlook Express, .pst folders for Outlook, and .pfc for AOL.

22. Click the **+** symbol next to the **baggifrodo** icon and the **baggifrodo** folder to see the AOL webmail folder structure located on this computer image. Click the **Away Messages** folder to see AOL Away Messages stored on this computer. Click each message, and view the text contained in each message in the lower file viewer window. Bookmark each message by clicking in each check box, right-click any checked message, and select **Create Bookmark**. In the Create New Bookmark dialog box, type **AOL Away Messages** in the Bookmark name text box, select the **All checked items**, check the **Include in report** and **Include parent of email attachments?** boxes, and click **OK**.

23. Click the **+** symbol next to the **Mail** folder to see the incoming and sent AOL message folders. Click the **Incoming/Saved Mail** folder, and select the first **Message0001** in the upper-right window to view the message. Check each box next to the messages; right-click the first message, select **Create Bookmark**, type **AOL Incoming Email** in the Bookmark name text box, select **All checked items**, check the **Include in report** and **Include parent of email attachments?** boxes, and click **OK**.

24. Click the **Mail You've Sent** folder, select each message for bookmarking, right-click any selected message, click **Create Bookmark**, type **AOL Sent Messages** in the Bookmark name text box, select **All checked items**, check the **Include in report** and **Include parent of email attachments?** boxes, and click **OK**.

15

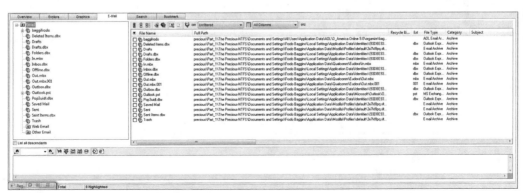

Figure 15-4   E-mail application folders

Course Technology/Cengage Learning

25. Click the **Inbox.dbx** icon, select each message, and create a bookmark named **Outlook Incoming Messages**; select **All checked items**, check the **Include in report** and **Include parent of email attachments?** boxes, and click **OK**.

26. Select the **Outlook.pst** folder, and click the **List all descendants** check box. The Outlook database folders, messages, notes, contacts, appointments, and tasks will be viewable in the upper-right window. Bookmark all the message files as **Outlook Messages**, select **All checked items**, check the **Include in report** and **Include parent of email attachments?** boxes, and click **OK**.

27. Click the **Search** tab, type **frodo** in the Search Term text box, and click **Add**. Type **keith** in the Search Term text box, click **Add**, and click **View Cumulative Results**. Click **OK** in the Filter Search Hits dialog box to look for any correspondence between Frodo Baggins and Keith. All messages between both suspects are listed in the bottom window, and notice the bookmarked messages in purple fonts. Select the second **Message0001** to view one of the messages between both suspects (see Figure 15-5).

28. Select the four additional unbookmarked messages, create a bookmark named **Frodo and Keith Messages**, select **All checked items**, check the **Include in report** and **Include parent of email attachments?** boxes, and click **OK**.

29. Click the **Overview** tab, and select the **Encrypted Files** bucket button to see the password-protected files located on this computer. Click the **double check box** icon on the left side of the middle tool bar, and in the FTK Confirmation dialog box, click **Yes** to select all the files. Right-click any file, select **Create Bookmark**, type **Encrypted Files** in the Bookmark name text box, select **All checked items**, check the **Include in report** and **Include parent of email attachments?** boxes, and click **OK**.

Figure 15-5 Correspondence

Course Technology/Cengage Learning

30. Click the **File** tab, select **Report Wizard**, and click **Next**. In the FTK Report Wizard – Bookmarks dialog box, select **Yes, include only bookmarks marked "Include in the report"** and **Yes, export all bookmarked files**, click **Next** six times, and click **Finish** in the FTK Report Wizard – Report Location dialog box. Click **Yes** in the Report Wizard dialog box to view the report. Close the report after you view it.

31. Leave all the windows open as you answer the review questions for this lab. Use the Search feature in FTK and the Registry Viewer to locate the answers to the information.

32. In the Registry Viewer, click the **File** tab, and select **Exit**. Click **Yes** in the Registry Viewer dialog box. Click the **File** tab in FTK, and select **Exit**. Click **No** in the FTK Exit Backup Confirmation dialog box.

Review Questions

1. What is the name of Frodo Baggins' company?

   a. Frodo Inc.

   b. Baggins Inc.

   c. Hobbytes Consulting

   d. Frodo Baggins Consulting

2. What appointment did Frodo keep on 2/2/2005?

   a. met with Keith

   b. met with Tara

   c. met with Mark

   d. met with Treebeard

3. On what day did the Southeast Cybercrime Summit open?

   a. July 8

   b. May 18

   c. February 28

   d. March 3

4. How many USB storage devices were attached to the seized computer?

   a. 1

   b. 6

   c. 5

   d. 4

5. When was the system registry file last written?

   a. 12/31/2004 21:51:27 UTC

   b. 10/25/2004 22:09:55 UTC

   c. 1/6/2005 21:30:33 UTC

   d. 12/17/2004 18:34:23 UTC

15

INDEX